Training Dogs

James O'Heare

GW00497874

BehaveTech Publishing

Ottawa, Canada

Title: Training Dogs
Publisher: BehaveTech Publishing, Ottawa, Canada,
www.BehaveTech.com
Author: James O'Heare
Cover art and book design: James O'Heare
Proof-reading: Kamrin MacKnight

Limits of Liability and Disclaimer of Warranty:

ISBN 978-1-927744-12-3

Preface

In this small book, I discuss some fundamental principles of behavior and some powerful strategies and tactics for managing dog behavior in a manner that is practical for the average dog owner. The principles, strategies, and tactics discussed here are derived directly from the natural science of behavior—behaviorology. These are not my own personal invention and they are not fads or gimmicks. The information in this book represents the most current science of behavior, shaped through many years of scientific work, stripped of pseudoscience. Thousands of pages could be written elaborating the principles and strategies found in this book, so the discussion here is merely the tip of the behavior training iceberg. Even though instructions are provided for specific training projects, you can treat these as examples. Simply adapt the principles, strategies, and tactics to any aspect of managing your dog's behavior or to train behaviors not described here. These same tools can be used to manage your spouse's, friend's, children's, parrot's, cat's, horse's, or even your own behavior. Use these principles, strategies, and tactics any time you seek to change the likelihood of a behavior.

This book introduces and uses some rather technical terms. It is important to use proper terms, as they have specific meanings, avoiding the confusion and misuse that typically plague colloquial language. For example, the word "reward" is *never* appropriate in the context of dog training. It does *not* mean the same thing as "reinforce," which has a specific unambiguous meaning, as described in this book. Furthermore, most colloquial terms suggest or imply a very nonscientific set of assumptions, which natural scientists are loath to support. Even though this book is intended for dog owners and not scientists, the use of proper terms is important for these reasons. In order to keep the contents accessible to most readers, a minimum number of technical terms are introduced and defined. Many of these terms are commonly used, such as "reinforce" and "punish." The reader is encouraged to use this technical vocabulary, as it will help reinforce the content of this book and proper repetition of the terms reinforces their proper use in general.

Thank you, Kamrin MacKnight for providing proof-reading services. Thank you, Debra Millikan for reviewing an early draft and providing valuable feedback, including a recommendation to include the fourth D-parameter. Thank you also to Stephen Ledoux for continuing to be a highly reinforcing mentor and colleague, which shows in all aspects of my writing and for reminding me to keep it simple. As always, any faults in this book are mine alone.

Table of Contents

Training Dogs

Introduction

This book is a bit different from many other books available on dog training. Rather than simply focusing on step-by-step instructions to train basic behaviors such as "sit" or "down," this book emphasizes that training occurs all of the time. Training happens any time that we are interacting with (or even ignoring) our dogs, not just in scheduled "training" sessions. This book details basic principles, strategies, and tactics that are based on the natural science of behavior. Step-by-step instructions are also provided, but the basic principles, strategies, and tactics are more important, as they are the tools needed to develop the generalized knowledge and skill to efficiently and effectively train any desired behavior. They can also help you understand how an undesirable became trained.

The natural science of behavior, behaviorology, seeks to explain behavior by identifying the functional relationship between observable/measurable behaviors and the natural events that control them. As a natural science, behaviorology does not speculate about non-natural inner forces, and is not concerned with intervening "cognitive" processes. Natural science only studies that which can be observed and measured. Natural science, does not, for instance, study the so-called "mind." Instead, behavior is studied for its own sake (as opposed to studying behavior merely as a window to the so-called "mind" or "soul"). Behavior is fully explained by events that set the occasion for it and then function as a consequence for that behavior. The natural science of behavior has identified many principles, indeed laws, of behavior, which are tested and confirmed on an ongoing basis. From these basic principles of behavior, behaviorologists (and behavior analysts) have devised powerful strategies and tactics for changing behavior. Highly effective practices and training protocols have been refined over the years.

By harnessing the products of the natural science of behavior, we are armed with the tools needed to thrive in non-coercive and mutually supportive relationships, and it is my hope that you will accept the challenge to apply these "tools" to promoting harmony, not only with your dog, but with others with whom you interact.

Behavior is always occurring and so is conditioning (sometimes colloquially called "learning"). Training should not be considered just

3

something we schedule in 5-minute sessions in order to get a dog to sit on cue. Though we may do this, we are well served by recognizing and taking advantage of everyday opportunities to train. That is, we are always training through all of our interactions with our dogs, whether or not we want/mean to, and this highlights that we can train more actively and intentionally. Relationships are not made up of just that small percentage of times we set aside to "work on them." They are made up of every interaction we share and that is also how we should view dog training.

Unlike most general dog training books, this book will take you on an intellectual journey, perhaps a challenging one at times. You will first explore the basic principles of behavior and strategies for changing behavior. Then, your knowledge will expand to encompass broad general strategies, as well as narrow tactics and specific practices. In addition, some step-by-step instructions for training common behaviors are provided. Familiarity with the natural science of behavior will arm you with the skills needed to (a) analyze why behaviors occur, and (b) change the behavior. These skills are useful in preventing and resolving problematic behaviors, as well as for training new behaviors. There are a great many books available that provide only step-by-step instructions to train specific behaviors. It is a bit more challenging to understand the abstract principles and strategies, but it is worth the effort because of the flexibility and adaptability it provides. An appreciation of the natural science behind the step-by-step instructions, provided in chapter 6, will condition in you the ability to respond more flexibly to training challenges and to devise your own step-by-step instructions for any new behaviors that you want to train. Chapter 6 also provides a basic set of steps that you can use to work through in training any behavior. You will find this to be beneficial in planning to train a behavior for which you do not have specific instructions. Command of the principles and strategies allows you to do what the professionals do: devise and implement plans to train anything. Once you have practiced the application of the principles and strategies to the behaviors provided here, you will be well-prepared for training new behaviors.

This is book one in the *Dog Behavior* series. Further books in this series will provide continued content related to living effectively with dogs. Book two will deal with resolving problematic dog behaviors.

One final note. This will *not* necessarily be an easy read. The information in this book is extremely powerful and worth the effort.

Ready it actively, rereading as necessary, rephrasing the concepts to yourself, generating your own examples and analyzing everyday behavior in proper scientific terms. Treat it like you would treat a textbook that you needed to pass a course with. If you get stuck, try to work it out, but if you cannot, proceed on and come back to that part at the end of that chapter, and perhaps it will make more sense in that context. Make use of the index as well to find and cross reference different concepts and terms. If you can put in the effort, the knowledge and skill you will harness will benefit you (and everyone around you) for the rest of your life, not just in living with dogs, but changing the behavior of others, including yourself. You'll get out what you put in.

I hope you enjoy the journey!

Training Dogs

Chapter 1. Basic Principles of Behavior

The natural science of behavior, behaviorology, seeks to explain behavior by identifying the functional relationship between observable behaviors and the events that control them. As a natural science, behaviorology does not speculate about non-natural inner forces and is not concerned with intervening "cognitive" processes. Instead, behavior is studied in its own right. Behavior is fully explained by events that set the occasion for it and then function as a consequence for that behavior. The natural science of behavior has identified many principles, indeed laws, of behavior, that are continually being tested and confirmed. From these basic principles of behavior, behaviorologists (and behavior analysts) have devised powerful strategies and tactics for changing behavior. Highly effective practices and training protocols have also been shaped over the years.

The following four principles explain the majority of behavior change processes important to training dogs. A principle of behavior is a statement that describes a relationship between a behavior and variables (i.e., "things") that control it. It is from such basic principles that strategies and tactics for changing behavior are derived.

Principle of Behavior #1. Behavior is Shaped by Consequences

This is also called the "Law of Effect" and involves a number of more specific principles. **Behavior** is simply (and complexly) a body's reaction to the environment. To change behavior, we make changes to the environment to which the body reacts. Some events/changes that occur immediately after a behavior make that behavior *more* likely in the future and some make it *less* likely. We call the stimuli that make behavior more likely, "**reinforcers**," and the ones that make behavior less likely, "**punishers**."

Reinforcement drives behavior, so this is generally where we focus our behavior changing efforts—either to strengthen a desirable behavior or to eliminate a problematic behavior. In the latter case, we avoid reinforcing the undesirable behavior, and instead, reinforce some other, more desirable, alternative behavior. But we'll get more into that strategy later. For now, just know that guesses don't determine what will reinforce or punish a behavior. Whether something is a reinforcer or a punisher (or neither) is decided by the actual changes, if any, that occur in the rate of that behavior after the consequence is instated. Typically, we can guess at what will be reinforcing or punishing, but sometimes, we are wrong. Be open to the possibility of being wrong by observing the actual rate of the behavior rather than relying too heavily on guesswork.

If a behavior is occurring, it means that there is a history of that behavior, at least sometimes, being reinforced. Try to get into the habit of always looking at what follows behavior and whether it increased the rate or likelihood of that behavior or decreased it. If you can get into this habit of analyzing what we call the "**contingencies**" (i.e., a behavior → consequence sequence), then you will understand why specific behaviors occur and will also have a good idea of how to change that behavior. After all, if some specific outcome is driving a behavior that you find problematic, then you can simply ensure that the consequence in question does not occur following that behavior. In fact, there are other strategies that help us get the behaviors we want without having to "extinguish" problem behaviors in this way since failing to reinforce a behavior is frustrating to the dog being trained.

More specifically, behavior is a product of *immediate* consequences. A stimulus introduced more than a couple seconds after a behavior will not affect that behavior. If you are going to reinforce a behavior, you need to do so immediately, ideally just as the behavior is being completed. This might involve simply praising the dog, giving a treat, or playing a quick game as soon as the behavior ends, or it can involve everyday reinforcers like placing a food bowl down, opening the back door, allowing the opportunity to sniff a fire hydrant etc. This also applies to punishers. We should always be focused on reinforcement over punishment, but just know that punishment delivered more than a couple seconds after the behavior won't work—it may well be punishing something else that the dog is doing at the time, such as looking at you or staying near you! At least being late with a reinforcer won't be harmful to your dog and your relationship.

You might have observed, at one point or another, that a dog has engaged in some "bad" behavior while the owners were away, and when the owners come home, the dog lowers his or her head, slinking away, evoking the word "guilty" from the owners. If so, you might be thinking that even after that long delay, the dog "knows" he did something wrong. Well, he or she may know they are in trouble, but they do not know they did something "wrong." In fact, this scenario is *not* an exception to our rule about immediate consequences. The dog is reacting fearfully in this example, not because of some so-called "knowledge" of past events and their "rightness" or "wrongness," but because the owner's return, in the context of some other stimuli, immediately elicits the fear. If previous instances of "punishment" worked, then the "bad" behavior would not have occurred. Instead, the behavior did occur, but the "guilt" is just "fear" and/or "appeasement." Attempting to punish a behavior that has occurred more than a couple seconds before will simply not work. Punishment will, however, cause a number of problems, including a deterioration in your relationship with your dog. Furthermore, it is unproductive to speculate about what a dog may or may not "know." We shall focus on behaviors we can observe directly.

In some contingencies (i.e., behavior → consequence sequence), a stimulus can be *added* immediately after the behavior or it can be *subtracted* after the behavior. Adding a treat to the situation after a behavior is likely to *in*crease the rate or likelihood of that behavior in the future. Adding a cuff-to-the-head after a behavior is likely to *de*crease the rate or likelihood of that behavior in the future (though this is never recommended and there are better ways to train, as explored in this book).

Stimuli can be subtracted, too. If a chain is hurting a dog's neck and walking closer to you *subtracts* (i.e., removes or decreases) that tightening and pain, then there will likely be an *in*crease in walking close to you in the future. Again, this type of pain-eliciting stimulation, also referred to as "**aversive**," generates a number of resilient and problematic side-effects that are best avoided by focusing on stimuli that elicit pleasure instead. Finally, if you are playing with a dog and *subtract* your play participation, contingent upon their teeth touching your skin, then the rate or likelihood of teeth touching your skin will likely *de*crease. Thus, there are four options of *adding* or *subtracting* the consequence and the resulting *increase* or *decrease* in the rate or likelihood of the behavior in the future. The following chart may be helpful in illustrating the distinctions described above.

Responding **Increases**

	Added Reinforcement **+R**	Subtracted Reinforcement **-R**	
Consequence Added	Added Punishment **+P**	Subtracted Punishment **-P**	Consequence Subtracted

Responding **Decreases**

Figure 1. The chart of consequences. + stands for "added" and − stands for "subtracted. P stands for "punishment" and R stands for "reinforcement."

There is one more outcome that affects the rate or likelihood of behavior—a fifth basic principle. If a behavior has been reinforced and you _withhold_ that reinforcement or prevent it from occurring, that will result in a _decrease_ in the rate or likelihood of that behavior. This is referred to as "**extinction**," as mentioned above. So, if barking and nudging has, at least sometimes, resulted in someone slipping the dog a piece of food at the dinner table, then discontinuing ever giving food at the table will result, eventually, in the elimination of that behavior.

To sum up, _adding a reinforcer after a behavior occurs will strengthen it and not adding that reinforcer after the behavior (extinction) will weaken it._ Though extinction is frustrating, and is best avoided where possible, it is important to understand that it works. Changing behavior for the better involves reinforcing desirable behaviors and not reinforcing undesirable behaviors. This book will help condition you to focus on added reinforcement and avoid extinction. But for now, it is important to always remember that _reinforcement drives behavior._ When it comes to purposely changing behavior, be that in training dogs or dealing with other people on a daily basis, the options that involve aversive stimuli (i.e., options other than added reinforcement) can cause more problems than they solve. It's far better to emphasize the use of added reinforcement for desirable behaviors.

The more you study the chart in figure 1, and think actively about the concepts by analyzing every-day real-life events and thinking up examples etc., the more effective and efficient you will be in analyzing episodes of behavior. But, if you take just the bare minimum away from this first law of behavior, let it be this: *behavior is maintained by consequences, some of which will make the behavior more likely, and some, less likely.* If you recognize this, you can control consequences and decide which behaviors will become more and less likely.

Principle of Behavior #2. Contingent Added Reinforcement Promotes Behavioral Well-being

This title has a few terms that need explaining. "**Added reinforcement**" refers to the *addition* of a consequence that results in an *increase* in the future rate or likelihood of the behavior it followed.

"**Contingent**" means that the reinforcer is added specifically based on certain criteria, in other words, it is delivered *contingent* (i.e., dependent) upon occurrence of the behavior in question.

Behavioral "well-being" is not a technical term and does not have a formal definition. It is usually subjectively defined, as a sense of satisfaction or contentment with one's circumstances. Behaviorally, it might relate to the presence of adaptive behaviors (i.e., acts that bring someone in contact with added reinforcers) and absence of maladaptive behavior, including those we might call "anxiety," "discomfort," or "pain." Even though behavioral well-being is subjective and ill-defined, it does represent real behaviors and a generally beneficial state of affairs, so it is still useful to consider it.

A common result of contact with aversive stimulation, particularly that which cannot be predicted and avoided, and an absence of contact with added reinforcers, tends to result in "response depression," which is characterized by an overall reduction in responding. This includes the problem situation referred to as "helplessness," characterized colloquially by giving up or shutting down. Helplessness involves a reduction in escape responses when an animal is faced with aversive stimulation (i.e., the animal has no opportunity to escape from the aversive stimulation). It can promote problematic behaviors such as self-mutilation or repetitive stereotypical behaviors.

11

By arranging an environment such that the dog contacts as many added reinforcers as possible and as few aversers as possible, one sets the occasion for behavioral well-being. One of the keys to really maximizing this effect is not just exposure to added reinforcers but making them *contingent* on appropriate and adaptive behaviors.

So, to promote behavioral well-being in dogs, the trainer needs to recognize useful behaviors and immediately reinforce them. This does not always just involve discrete behaviors such as sitting quietly and calmly before going outside or getting dinner. It can mean exhibiting behaviors characterized as "persistent" or working through frustration, rather than shutting down. In some instances, it may involve behaviors that we might refer to as being particularly "creative," in finding novel, but productive solutions. These general behavior tendencies can be reinforced just as other, more discrete, behaviors like "sit." If you make added reinforcers contingent upon particularly useful behaviors or patterns of behavior, they will increase in likelihood. This allows the dog to access a greater number of highly effective added reinforcers overall, allowing the dog to benefit from the beneficial emotional reactions that come with this contact with added reinforcers.

Principle of Behavior #3. Aversive Consequences Generate Insidious Side-effects

In his classic book, *Coercion and its Fallout*, (2001), Dr. Sidman outlines the many insidious and resilient problematic side-effects that aversive stimulation generates. Of particular concern is aversive stimulation that is intense and unpredictable/unavoidable. However, moderately intense aversive stimulation that is predictable and avoidable can also generate these side-effects. Nor is it a matter of whether the punitive methods are carried out improperly or not. The problematic side-effects are an inherent component of the effects of contacting and reacting to aversive stimulation. The only reason we use the word "side" in side-effects is because they are not the "desired" effects.

Harsh aversive stimulation can generate problematic emotional reactions, which can then generalize quite readily, meaning that other things present when exposed to it come to also elicit these problematic emotional behaviors. This can get out of hand very quickly. For example, if someone jerks on a dog's leash, causing pain to the dog, the presence of a leash alone, under any circumstance, might come to elicit a pain reaction (and in the absence of the original physical impact, we might refer to it as a "fearful reaction"). The jerk doing the jerking may also come to elicit fear. The feelings that these emotional behaviors generate can be extremely unpleasant and they tend to be persistent and resistant to change.

Aversive stimulation also generates escape behaviors. Sometimes, these escape behaviors become problematic. In some cases, they involve what we would call "aggressive" behaviors (note that escape does not mean just running away; it means whatever reduces—*subtracts*—the aversive stimulation). It can even generate self-mutilation behaviors. Some escape behaviors are called "counter-control" because they function to "control the controller," as Sidman puts it. Again, these can become problematic behaviors themselves that are very resistant to change.

Some techniques are more aversive than others and are more likely to generate such problematic effects. For example, extinction within the context of providing access to the reinforcer in question with other more acceptable behaviors is minimally aversive and less likely to cause problems than unpredictable beatings. However, as a general policy, it is best to try to avoid using *any* kind of aversive stimulation. It is best to emphasize added reinforcement of desirable behaviors.

Principle of Behavior #4. Behavior is Continuous and Conditioning is Always Occurring

Behavior is continuous. That means that behavior is always occurring. Some behaviors are so fleeting or involve extremely small movements that you may not even see them, while others are continuous and may be recognized because they continue to occur rather than begin and end discretely. For example, standing is a behavior in general and it is made up of a number of smaller balance maintaining related behaviors. Large scale behaviors (e.g., running or walking) are easily recognized but smaller scale, or more subtle behaviors (e.g., shifting weight to balance while standing), may not be recognized for what they are: behaviors. Nevertheless, behaviors are always occurring and all of them are subject to reinforcement, punishment, and extinction on an ongoing basis.

Chapter 2. Proactive Behavior Shaping Strategies

In this chapter and the next, some general strategies for managing and shaping the behavior of dogs toward the goal of promoting a more harmonious relationship between the people and dogs living together are described. These strategies are derived from the basic principles of behavior described in the chapter 1, and have been shaped by the hard work of behaviorologists, behavior analysts, and behavior technologists over many years. These methods provide us, not only general approaches to training dogs to sit and come when called and the like, but how to support desirable behavior on a moment-by-moment basis, thereby supporting the mutually reinforcing social relationship between people and their dogs. It also helps us deal with our own behavior and that of others. As you will see, many of the strategies are related and overlap, which is good, because they complement each other.

Several strategies for promoting desirable behaviors in dogs and living harmoniously with them were hinted at in chapter 1. This chapter focuses on *proactive* strategies for training. Chapter 3 covers *reactive* strategies.

Proactive Strategy #1. Maintain Consistency for Efficient and Effective Training

Consistency refers to establishing simple and clear rules, and ensuring that they are maintained at all times. If a dog is allowed on the bed sometimes and not others, the complex rule governing the exceptions (assuming there is even a consistent rule) may not be adequately conditioned (referred to as "discrimination training"). The rule should consistently be both clear and simple. If the dog must sit until released when food bowls are being put down, then requiring that usually, as opposed to always, is going to cause "errors" without some very specialized training beyond the scope of this book (or the interest of most dog owners). Dogs are required to get up to speed on human rules pretty quickly and then to abide by them, all without the benefit of language. It is surely tough enough without also having to try to figure out the complex rules of exceptions. Keep the rules simple! You might indeed want to allow exceptions under certain specific circumstances but it is best to avoid doing this where possible. Importantly, if the exceptions are based on your mood, then it becomes impossible for the training to be effective. This will likely lead to problem behaviors and discord between you and your dog.

Rules usually define what *not* to do. This can be a problem since there is an almost infinite number of things one ought not do, but one will, of course, always be doing *something*. It is more productive and efficient is to define what one *is to do*. So, while rules defining what *not* to do are fine, thought should also be given, in each instance, as to what one would prefer the dog did *instead* to access the reinforcer that would maintain the problem behavior for which a rule became necessary. In other words, if a dog is not to sleep on the bed, then how exactly is the dog to seek comfort? A very comfortable option should be made available, perhaps one with privacy and one in the thick of family life. Or, why not just let the dog sleep on the bed? If a dog is not to be gobbling food out of the bowl as you try to fill it, then he or she should sit instead (or frill it on the counter). If the dog is not to pull on leash, then he or she should walk close to the handler. In each case, there is an alternative. The dog can access the reinforcer, just with a desirable rather than an undesirable behavior. If the rule is consistent and the dog is set up to exhibit the acceptable behavior right off the bat, the problem is prevented or solved.

In all cases, the reinforcer must be considered. Indeed, it's all about the reinforcers! If the dog seeks comfort, then that can be made available, contingent upon the desired behavior rather than any problematic behavior. Likewise, if the dog seeks food, then sitting should result in feeding, while barging should not. If the dog seeks to access a fire hydrant or to run free, perhaps opportunities to access a fire hydrant or run should be made available, contingent upon walking nicely on leash first or sitting while the leash is removed and coming when called.

These examples illustrate the need to focus on what the dog *is to do* rather than what he or she is *not to do*. One needs to accurately identify the reinforcer involved in situations where appropriate or inappropriate behaviors might occur and then make consistent rules to define, not only what the dog should not do, but what the dog *can* do in order to access the reinforcer in question.

Set reasonable, clear, and unambiguous rules, and then endeavor to arrange the environment in order to support the desirable behaviors, frequently taking the opportunity to immediately reinforce desirable behaviors. If you can implement the strategy outlined in this one paragraph, you will have set yourself up for success!

Proactive Strategy #2. Control Added Reinforcers and Use Them to Your (*Everyone's*) Advantage.

One of the most effective strategies for controlling dog behavior is to take control of added reinforcers. Obviously, treats are one option, but many other things can also function as added reinforcers. Playing with a dog, or providing a toy that the dog may play with on their own can be reinforcing, as can placing the food bowl down, going out for a walk, meeting other dogs or people, sniffing fire hydrants and running off leash (but the list goes on and on). You can identify added reinforcers by it being what the dog will behave in order to get access to—that is, what the dog expends energy accessing. Taking control of these reinforcers simply means controlling when the dog may access them. Once you have that control, you can provide reinforcers contingent upon desirable behaviors, either those that you cue or are cued by some other part of the environment (e.g., the presence of a leash or agility equipment).

It is important to remember that added reinforcers such as treats and toys are not always necessarily reinforcing. Their capacity to be reinforcing will be conditional upon how much and how recent access to the reinforcer was. For example, if you eat a large meal, then food won't be very reinforcing for a while, and it might even be aversive during that interval. If a toy has been continuously available recently, it may be less effective as a reinforcer than if it had not been recently available. Less or less recent access is referred to as "deprivation" and more or more recent access is referred to as "satiation." When satiated, the stimulus is less effective as a reinforcer and won't help you much in training.

This is **_not_** to recommend a boot-camp type of arrangement! It is okay to provide or allow "free" reinforcers, but just don't forget to use some everyday reinforcers to your advantage. You might want to cue a behavior sometimes, like sit, before the dog is allowed to eating or go outside, but you might also simply recognize desirable behaviors as they occur and take that opportunity to praise and toss a treat or have a quick game of tug. Control can be excessive—Don't overdo it.

Proactive Strategy #3. Errorless Training: Arrange the Environment to Make Desirable Behaviors Likely and Problematic Behaviors Unlikely (Set the Dog Up for Success).

Colloquially, an "error" seems to hold a moral component and anyone committing an "error" is at "fault" or is deficient in some way. This is not how scientists use the term, and indeed, most behaviorologists and behavior analysts cringe at the use of this word, which was coined quite some time ago when natural scientists of behavior were less careful about the terms they used. Historically, in a behavioral sense, the word "error" refers to non-criterion behaviors (i.e., undesirable behaviors that occur after some program has been put in place to support a more desirable behavior). So, if you have been training a dog to sit, you say "sit," and the dog fails to sit, that would be an "error," or non-criterion behavior (because the behavior fails to meet the criteria for "sit"). There is no "fault" involved, but let's move on to what is most important about this strategy.

In the past, training was handled in more or less a "trial-and-error" manner in which the subject was "free" to exhibit whatever behaviors occurred without any proactive management (i.e., "antecedent control") and rules were set to select from all of these behaviors—to reinforce acceptable behavior and to punish or extinguish unacceptable behaviors. In this way, one simply picked and chose, and the dog's repertoire of behavior "evolved," or was "shaped" in a manner of speaking.

The problem with this approach is that there will be many "errors" and hence there will be many aversive experiences, as those "errors" are eliminated from the subject's repertoire. There is a better way to "shape" behavior. A paradigm shift has involved recognizing that these "errors" are not necessary in order for the behavior to be shaped. We do not have to sit back and select from whatever behaviors happen to occur. This older "eliminative" paradigm has been replaced with a "constructional" paradigm (Goldiamond, 1974/2002). Under this new paradigm, using an "errorless training strategy," the rule is still set to reinforce desirable behaviors and fail to reinforce problematic behaviors,

18

but instead of just selecting from whatever behaviors occur, we proactively manipulate the environment in such a way that the desirable behavior is *more* likely to occur (in some cases, is the only behavior possible), and problem behaviors are *least* likely to occur (or are even impossible). The trainer works to put the dog in a position to succeed, or put another way, the dog is set up for success.

Here is generally how this is achieved. First, the appropriate behavior (e.g., sit) and inappropriate behaviors (e.g., jumping up, running, or anything other than sitting even) are identified. Then, changes are made to the environment that support the likelihood of the desirable behavior occurring instead of any problem behaviors. For example, distractions are reduced and training time is selected by when the dog has the least "pend up" energy, and when the dog is most hungry if you are using treats in the training. When the desirable behavior occurs, it is immediately reinforced, every single time at first. When the desirable behavior occurs reliably, the reinforcers are delivered on a gradually and slowly thinning schedule, always making sure the schedule is rich enough to support the behavior and keep it going. Finally, any arrangements (i.e., things or practices that you put in place to promote desirable over undesirable behaviors) that cannot be maintained are gradually faded out. For example, you may gradually introduce distractions and train at more energetic times or when the dog is not necessarily hungry. By that time, there is a solid history of added reinforcement for the desirable behavior, leaving the undesirable behaviors unlikely to occur at all. Why would these other behaviors occur when the desirable/criterion behavior is so clearly effective?

If you do not want the dog jumping up on the counter looking for food, you can manage the environment by *never* having food accessible on the counter. Then, you can reinforce behaviors such as the dog sitting and just waiting patiently by giving them dinner. Or, if you do not want the dog chewing up shoes, ensure that shoes are *never* accessible, but simultaneously ensure that appropriate chew toys are *readily* available. Chewing the toys will be intrinsically reinforcing, but you can still "catch the dog doing something right" and provide praise and a treat as well. Later, you can introduce the *possibility* of "errors" and continue to develop a strong history of reinforcement for the desirable behavior, meaning, eventually you should be able to leave some shoes out and they will not get destroyed. But, don't rush it!

At some point, you might find that some degree of management is required on a long-term basis or that a refresher needs to be instated. But, in general, if you can think and plan proactively, you can get the training done with few or no "errors."

"Errors" can occur of course, even under well thought-out training plans. If they happen, it becomes necessary to become reactive instead, as addressed in chapter 4.

Proactive Strategy #4. Graded Training: Break Complex Tasks Down into Smaller, More Manageable, Tasks.

"Graded" training involves (a) breaking projects down into smaller more manageable steps or projects that can be worked separately and in an appropriate order, and (b) arranging exposure to stimuli along dimensions such as distance, duration, distraction, and diversity of environments. It involves reducing the level of difficulty in whatever way supports success and then increasing difficulty at a pace that ensures success. For example, if you want to train a dog to lie on a mat, it is best to train "going to the mat" and "lying down on the mat" separately and then link them together after the dog reliably exhibits the individual behaviors on cue. It might also mean starting training in a minimally distracting environment and only when the new behavior is reliable, very gradually increasing the level of distraction, but only at a pace that ensures the behavior remains reliable. This applies to changes in duration, distance, and diversity of environments as well, what we usually call the "4 Ds" or the "D-parameters," as discussed in chapter 9.

Any time that training a task seems unwieldy, find a way to break it down into incremental steps that you can separately train. Or, if a given environment makes training difficult, manage it in a way that makes the task easier and then gradually return the environment to what can be expected "in the real world."

As an extended example, if you want your dog to sit at the door before being let outside, first train a good solid sit just for treats. Then, consider letting the dog be outside for a while (remember satiation to reduce the effectiveness of a reinforcer and hence reduce the likelihood of rushing out the door). Then, when you return inside, try requesting the sit at the door right away. Instead of being super excited to go out, making the sit unlikely, the dog will be only moderately excited to go out and you are more likely to get the sit. Then, open the door (closing it if the dog breaks position), and expecting the dog to hold the position only very briefly, as soon as it is near opened, release the dog as reinforcement for sitting. You can gradually work up the duration of the sit later and you can slowly reduce the level of deprivation (i.e., time since he or she has been out) as well. You might even come in and not close the door completely at first, making it even less likely that the dog will rush out when opened more widely. The tactics discussed in chapter 4 further elucidate this process.

Proactive Strategy #5. Take Every Conditioning Opportunity to Train

Recall Principle #4—behavior is continuous. This implies that there are always opportunities, at every moment, for training of appropriate or inappropriate behaviors. We can support our training goals or sabotage them, depending upon how we handle the situations. We might even miss the opportunity to participate in training, if we do not recognize that behavior is continuous. Training is not something one just schedules and then carries out for 15 minutes each day and is then neglected through the rest of the day. Indeed, one may arrange specific times in which to engage in intensive and goal-specific training, but conditioning is occurring *all the time* and *any* interaction with a dog involves numerous instances of conditioning (i.e., training) like it or not. If one focuses only on specific training sessions, they might counter that training at other times. In any given day, you might be able to just go about your normal business and achieve many times the amount of training that you achieved in a daily 15 minute "training session," just by taking advantage of the myriad of opportunities to fit in a training trial here and there as these opportunities emerge.

One of my favorite dog training books is *Train Your Dog the Lazy Way* by Andrea Arden, in which dog owners are encouraged to take every opportunity to train their dogs during day-to-day life. If your interaction involves, or could involve, a reinforcer of any kind, you should take that opportunity to at least ensure that appropriate behaviors, and not inappropriate behaviors, are being exhibited at that time. In addition, you should consider strengthening a cue (such as "sit" for instance). If you are going to hand out a potato chip while watching TV, at least ensure that the dog is being "politely" attentive rather than "obnoxiously" attentive. On top of that, consider asking for a "sit" if the initial training for that behavior has already been done. In fact, over time, you should be able to drop the vocal cue and the context of waiting for a chip will cue the behavior itself! As alluded to, any given behavior at any moment may result in some environmental event that functions as a reinforcer or punisher, or a previously available reinforcer might not occur, resulting in an extinction trial.

Think like a behaviorologist and recognize every behavior and what follows it, and the functional relation between those two events. If you are able to control what occurs immediately following a behavior, ensure that you are reinforcing desirable behaviors and failing to reinforce problematic behaviors at all times, not just during designated "training sessions." Recall Proactive Strategy #2 as well (and take note of Reactive Behavior Shaping Strategy #2 in the next chapter).

If a problem behavior has occurred, that means you have to become reactive rather than proactive, and in this situation, analyze why you failed to maintain an errorless approach, so that you can avoid such errors in the future.

Proactive Strategy #6. Make Training "Fun" for All Concerned

Sometimes we need to remind ourselves that even though training is important, be it for vital tasks such as coming when called or walking on loose leash, behaviors for which we might arrange specific training sessions, or just requesting a sit before you toss the dog a chip while watching TV, that the only way the training is going to work is if participation is reinforcing for both you and the dog. That is, if training of any kind is not "fun," the dog will shut down, ignore you, exhibit inappropriate behaviors, or perhaps grudgingly comply and lead to the emergence of problematic side-effects, resulting, at the very least, in slower training. This will likely generate frustration on your part, which will make the entire process even less fun and the relationship will suffer as a result, perhaps leading things to quickly spiral out of control.

A strong harmonious relationship is built on added reinforcers. Why not have fun in training? If you apply the basic principles and use sound training strategies, especially the proactive ones discussed to this point, you will be in the best possible position to experience fun. The victories you achieve in your training and improved relationship will function to reinforce your efforts. However, things can get frustrating from time to time. The best thing to do in these situations is to avoid engaging in training while you are frustrated or upset. Manage the situation, so that training is not required at that specific time and then come back to it after you are exhibiting a better "mood."

Be careful not to allow problem behaviors to end training. If you reinforce some kind of disruptive behavior that ends a less than fun training session, that is exactly what you will see more often. To avoid this problem, (a) avoid allowing training to occur that is less than fun, and (b) if training seems to be deteriorating, perhaps just because it is going on too long, get and reinforce a few occurrences of a behavior that is fun, quick, and easy, that you know will occur with a high degree of confidence and then end the session. By ending the session on a positive note by reviewing a quick and easy behavior (like perhaps a couple sit–down pushups), you reduce the risk of encouraging disruptive behaviors. Plus, both you and your dog will be happier.

Make training fun by being happy and enthusiastic yourself, maintaining a fun and stimulating pace, using lots of effective reinforcers and avoiding excessive frustration, aversive stimulation, and excessively long or challenging training sessions. Ensure that you are reinforcing at least every 5 to 10 seconds.

Training Dogs

Chapter 3. Reactive Behavior Shaping Strategies

The proactive approach is always preferable, but now and then, problematic behaviors occur, in spite of our efforts to preclude or replace them. The strategies in this chapter are damage control for when proactive strategies fail.

Reactive Strategy #1. Differential Reinforcement—The Extinction Side of the Coin

"Differential reinforcement" is the name of a procedure used extensively in behaviorology and behavior analysis. Loosely, it refers to two rules being in place at the same time. One rule identifies a behavior of interest that is to be additively reinforced when it occurs (with or without your prompting it). The other rule states that other behaviors occurring in that same context instead of the behavior of interest (the "problem" behavior) are to be extinguished.[1] Much of this process is accomplished with the proactive approach, but even though we try to avoid occurrence of the problematic behavior, it might occasionally occur and in those situations, we need some way to deal with it. Recall that extinction involves preventing reinforcement for a behavior from occurring. When a problematic behavior occurs, it is vital that it not be reinforced.

Behaviors that are reinforced occasionally and seemingly randomly, tend to persist. Think of it this way. If you put money into a vending machine and the reinforcer (your drink or food item) is not forthcoming, your likelihood of engaging in more money-inserting behavior would likely end quickly and completely. If, on the other hand,

---

[1] This is actually a differential reinforcement-like procedure. Strictly speaking, the behavior of concern and the problem behavior must be members of the same response class for the procedure to be differential reinforcement. That means that both behaviors must contact the same reinforcer—called the "functional reinforcer." However, in animal training circles, the term differential reinforcement is common used where the behavior of concern and the problem behavior do not necessarily share the same reinforcer. Acknowledging this distinction, I will proceed maintaining the term "differential reinforcement" to refer to this differential reinforcement-like procedure.

you insert money into a slot machine and the reinforcer (money being won) is not forthcoming, your likelihood of money-inserting behavior is likely to remain strong, even if the reinforcer is rare. This illustrates the difference between the persistence of behavior maintained on a continuous schedule and one maintained on what we call an "intermittent schedule," specifically, a "variable ratio schedule."

A behavior that never generates a reinforcer is unlikely to occur at all. So, if you prevent a problem behavior from being reinforced, it will cease to occur. If, on the other hand, the problematic behavior occurs and you allow it to be reinforced even rarely (or you are not even aware that you have reinforced it), the behavior will persist and strongly so. Think of the counter-surfing dog that just occasionally finds some nice food up there.

In fact, the scenario gets worse. If you fail to reinforce a behavior that was once reinforced, it will typically occur a bit more strongly, quickly, loudly etc. for a little while, a product of frustration. We call this an "extinction burst." Think of a vending machine that "eats your coins." You might push or hit the machine or curse at it; your behavior becomes suddenly variable and more forceful. Think of the person who pushes the elevator button and the door does not open soon enough so the person pushes the button a number of times quickly and with more pressure— that's more variation, occasioned by the frustration of extinction. If you reinforce a particularly intense variation of the behavior, that is what you will have shaped. The problem behavior will then be even *more* problematic. It will likely be exhibited with more force or higher volume or at a higher rate in a bout. This is how extreme tantrums are shaped in children begging for candy in grocery store checkout lines. The parents try to hold out, but the child's tantrum gets too embarrassing (aversive) for them and they give in to the child, shaping a more intense version of the request for candy. Therefore, it is vital that any problematic behavior, once identified as such, not be reinforced at all—*ever*. Furthermore, if a behavior is extinguished quickly by ensuring it is never reinforced, the frustration it generates will also be quickly extinguished. A protracted extinction process due to "eventually giving in" will result in even more frustration in the dog (and yourself). It is not fun for the child to exhibit tantrum behavior; it is unpleasant for all concerned. You do no one any favors, least of all the dog, by finally slipping the dog a piece of food at the dinner table when they nudge your arm one too many times.

Some behaviors generate reinforcement "automatically" (i.e., endogenously), in a way that you cannot control. For instance, barking may be reinforced by extrinsic sources, but sometimes, it also generates a powerful automatic reinforcement inside the dog's body. It may result in the release of cortisol, endorphins, or adrenaline, which function to reinforce the behavior (barking "feels good"). You cannot control this kind of reinforcement and so a proactive approach becomes even more important in these kinds of cases. In some cases, you can do what we refer to as "chain interruption." In this procedure, you stop the behavior as early in the sequence as possible, ideally right when incipient motions are noticed (i.e., when the dog is just getting ready to exhibit the behavior). This approach minimizes the amount of reinforcement that is contacted. This is not always possible, and physically stopping a behavior is *not* ideal either, as it is likely to be aversive and result in problematic side-effects.

Reactive Strategy #2. Identify Why the Proactive Strategy Failed and Adjust as Needed

The other major task to carry out when a problem behavior does occur, is for you to analyze why it occurred and why you failed to proactively control it. Then, you can fix that problem so it is less likely to occur again. What "evoked" (i.e., triggered) the behavior? Did you not realize that this stimulus was evocative of the behavior? Did you know, but you simply failed to control its occurrence? When you know this, you should be able to find a way to proactively arrange the environment, making this mistake less likely to occur in the future.

Chapter 4. Training Tactics

Whereas "principles" describe functional relations and strategies are broad, general, approaches to a problem, "tactics" are more specific. While tactics are not yet specific one-off examples, they are more specific to application than strategies. We can think of them as "general procedures." The tactics described here are presented more or less in the order in which they are applied, with a little overlap in some cases. These tactics are most applicable to specific goal-directed training sessions (like training the dog to "sit" on cue), but they can prove useful in serendipitous training as well.

Training Tactic #1. When Training a Specific Behavior, Be Clear About the Behavior

Often, it is enough to recognize appropriate behaviors and reinforce them, and recognize problem behaviors and fail to reinforce them, trying to make them less likely to occur in the future. However, especially when we are training very specific behaviors like sit or down, coming when called, or walking on loose leash etc., it is a good idea to have a very specific set of criteria for that behavior, to ensure that it remains consistent. Does "sit" mean only putting the butt on the ground? What if the front elbows are on the ground too? Then it's a down and not a sit. You do not always necessarily have to have some description so detailed that it looks like a legal contract, but you do have to know what will trigger your giving a treat and what will not. The more specific and consistent you are, the better. Give some thought to behaviors you train and ensure specificity and consistency; don't allow the criteria to shift over time.

Training Tactic #2. Identify Your Dog's Top Reinforcers

All dogs are different. Some dogs will work for treats and others won't. Some dogs will work forever just for praise, but most will not. A quick game of tug might be an effective reinforcer for some dogs and a chore for others (one subtractively reinforced just by getting it over with). In fact, some dogs will work just for the opportunity to keep working with you, and other reinforcers only serve to take them away from the fun. It is important that we not impose our opinions onto what is and is not an effective reinforcer for an individual dog. Observe what your dog commonly does work for and not, in order to identify what actually does reinforce their behavior. That is, if you provide it following a behavior, and the behavior becomes much more likely than before, then it is a reinforcer. It's all about the rate or likelihood of the behavior and not about what we feel should be a reinforcer. Make a list of your dog's top five effective reinforcers in rank order. This will make training much more effective and efficient.

Training Tactic #3. Use Motivating Operations

A "motivating operation" is something you do that temporarily makes the reinforcer either more or less effective than it was in the past and hence makes the behavior more likely at that time. In most cases, we want to increase the effectiveness of a reinforcer, and this means deprivation. We are **_not_** talking about some terrible horror movie in which you eliminate everything fun from the dog's life and dole out the fun only for compliance! One must be very careful with deprivation. If you are thinking a little deprivation improves the reinforcer then a lot must improve it a ton, then you are wrong!

What this means is that it will be better to train before dinner rather than right afterward, if you're using food treats as a reinforcer. It might also mean rotating access to toys so that some are available and other are kept out of sight for a while or are only accessible during training sessions. Then, when you bring those toys out, they will instantly be the most valuable toys in the place, and hence the most effective reinforcers. If the dog has not been outside in a while, then getting to go out will likely be more effective as a reinforcer than if they had just been outside for quite some time. Smelling a fire hydrant might be a highly effective reinforcer before and when they begin investigating it, but the longer they investigate it, the less effective it becomes.

You should generally not withhold social contact from dogs, but certainly appreciate that with some dogs more than others, they might become satiated with such contact and hence it can become less effective as a reinforcer than it would otherwise be. If you are always like the abominable snowman in the Bugs Bunny Show, and you "love him and squeeze him and call him George," social attention might not be high on the list of reinforcers for a little while.

Just be aware that satiation can make a reinforcer *less* effective and mild deprivation can make it *more* effective. But, be careful with this!

Training Tactic #4. Prompt Behaviors so That You May Then Reinforce Them

In order to train a behavior, it must occur so that you may then reinforce it. Sometimes, behaviors don't occur frequently on their own (e.g., those cued by some part of the environment other than you). In this situation, you need to generate the behavior first. Helping to get the behavior to occur is called "prompting." One of the most powerful forms of prompting is called "luring" or "targeting." You might hold a small piece of treat in your fingers, let the dog smell it, and then move it in a way that, as they try to keep smelling it closely, the behavior happens. For example, you might bring it just over the dog's head and they may sit in order to keep tracking the treat. Or, you might move your hand with the treat in it around the dog's body, so that he or she turns in a circle to keep tracking the treat, producing a spin. You can use luring with a treat to get a great many behaviors to occur. As soon as the behavior occurs, you may reinforce it by giving the dog the treat.

Training Tactic #5. Fade Prompts

If you use prompts, you need to fade them rather quickly because if you do not, then they might become a necessary element of the cue for the behavior. In other words, if you always lure a sit with the treat, and then you discontinue holding the treat "up front," the dog likely won't exhibit the behavior until you do so.

This is particularly important if you use the reinforcer you will provide them as part of the prompt (i.e., if you feed the dog the treat that you used to lure them with). In this case, once you have lured the behavior and reinforced a few times in a row, try luring as before, but this time, without the treat in your hand. When the behavior occurs, deliver a treat quickly (have treats hidden in a treat-pouch on your belt behind your back). Then ping-pong around, gradually increasing the number of times the treat is not in your hand, in a seemingly random manner, until you no longer hold the treats in your hand at all. Because the dog is conditioned to exhibit the behavior by getting the treats, regardless of whether you had the treats in your hand or not while you're cueing, the behavior will be trained quickly and easily, and you will have avoided the behavior becoming "treat dependent." This common problem has led to criticism of using treats in training, but the problem is based, not on the use of treats, but their incorrect use.

Even if you don't use a treat in your hand, but use some other kind of prompt (e.g., pointing at a mat to encourage the dog to go to the mat), you still need to fade these as well, unless you want to keep that prompt as a cue. In this case, gradually, over several trials, make the prompt less and less prominent/salient until it is gone all together and the behavior occurs anyway. If it is faded gradually, the behavior will continue to occur.

If the prompt is visual, then it is faded in terms of how it looks. If the prompt is auditory, such as when you make little high-pitched sounds to get a puppy to come to you, then you fade the prompt in terms of volume or the duration of the sounds etc.

The trick in all of these cases, is to eliminate the prompts, as they were only helpers, and you don't necessarily want these helpers to become established components of the cue.

In some cases, you might want a hand signal as your cue after that or you might want a vocal cue, as described next.

Training Tactic #6. Put a Cue on Behaviors

The rule: Only attach a permanent cue to a behavior once (a) it is exhibited at least close to the way you want it, and (b) you are sure it will occur after you deliver the cue.

You can still refine the form, latency, and speed a bit once the cue is established, as we will discuss below, but don't try to establish the indefinite cue for a behavior until you are pretty sure the behavior will occur within a few seconds of your giving the current cue or prompt. If you give the cue and the behavior does not happen, that is a setback in establishing the cue.

You will likely have been prompting the behavior at first, either with noises or gestures or luring/targeting. You will want to transfer control of the behavior from the prompt to a permanent/indefinite (or temporary even) cue, as described below.

If the prompt you used and the cue you seek to establish are similar enough, you can gradually and incrementally make the prompt seem more like the cue with each trial until the dog responds appropriately to the cue itself (called "prompt fading"). For example, if you were luring a sit and you already faded the treats from your hand, but you are still getting the behavior with the luring motion and you want to use a hand signal, then with each trial, make the lure motion look a little less like the lure motion and a little more like the hand signal. If the approximation is small enough, the dog will continue to respond appropriately throughout these trials and the hand signal will take control over the behavior. One common hand signal for sit, while we are on the topic, is holding your arm straight down, bend the elbow so the hand (upper arm remaining in place), palm up, raised upward toward your face (all the way or just half way).

That tactic will not work as well if the prompt and cue are too dissimilar. For instance, if you want to transfer control from the hand signal to a vocal cue, that will require a different tactic (called "prompt delay"). To transfer control from a prompt to a cue that is quite dissimilar, follow this sequence:

New cue → Old cue or prompt → Behavior → Reinforcer

Repeat several times and then delay giving the old cue/prompt to determine whether the new one alone will evoke the behavior. If so, great, and if not, repeat for several more trials and try again. For example, to transfer control of sit from the hand signal to a vocal cue, deliver the new cue "sit," followed by the hand signal, which generates the behavior, which you then reinforce with a treat. Do this several times, and then after saying "sit" one time, wait a few seconds to see if the sitting behavior occurs without the hand signal. It likely will, partly just because of the repetition momentum and partly because of the "pairing" procedure you just did. After reinforcing that and a few more times with just the new cue, that new cue takes on good solid control over the behavior.

In most cases, you will not be sure that the behavior will occur after a cue until you have done quite a bit of initial training to get it reliable. In that kind of situation, the cue is added later in the training process. In some cases, you can be sure that the behavior will occur within a couple seconds of giving the cue, and in those cases, you may establish the cue right away. The rule in all such cases of establishing a cue is to deliver the cue, get the behavior, and then reinforce it. When, and if, you are quite sure the behavior will occur, you are free to start delivering the to-be-trained cue. We have now covered this rule: Do not give the cue unless you are quite sure the behavior will occur right away.

Here is another rule: Do not repeat the cue. If the dog does not exhibit the behavior after you deliver the cue, (a) do not deliver the treat and (b) generally provide as little stimulation of any kind for a few seconds, followed by (c) cuing an "easier" behavior, if need be, or another opportunity to exhibit the behavior of interest on cue, perhaps this time with a prompt to ensure it occurs. Extinction, used in conjunction with a constructive means of getting back on track is minimally aversive. However, this should generally be avoided in favor of not using a cue unless you are sure the behavior will occur. If you start getting more than a few rare instances of non-criterion behavior, you are clearly pushing too hard, too fast. Back up and proceed more slowly.

Back to the rule. One reason we do not repeat the cue is because you have already created a trial in which the cue is not paired with the behavior. If you repeat the cue, you repeat that same sabotaging conditioning. If, by some chance, the behavior does occur after some number of cue-deliveries, you condition the dog to wait for that cue sequence. In other words, the cue to sit, becomes "sit, sit, sit" and the dog will not exhibit the behavior until the third "sit" is vocalized. It's true, the dog will wait for that third "sit," if that is how you condition it.

Training Tactic #7. Thin the Schedule of Reinforcement

Initially, it is always best to reinforce every single instance of a behavior you are training. This ensures that there is a strong increase in the rate of the behavior. However, this is tough to keep up in real life in the long-run. Perhaps more importantly, the behavior will tend to extinguish quickly and easily, if you cannot keep up the continuous reinforcement schedule.

Remember the vending machine versus the slot machine? As soon as the behavior is fairly reliable, try failing to reinforce one trial and quickly cue the behavior again and reinforce that one. It is highly doubtful that the behavior will fail to occur based on that one single extinction trial but what will have been conditioned is that "reinforcers are not available every single time, but keep trying and it will occur again" and the behavior becomes a little bit more resilient. Very gradually, in a seemingly random manner, increase the number of trials that do not result in reinforcement. So, do a couple more with reinforcement and then one without, and then do three with and one without, and then do one with and one without, and then do two with and two without, and then do three with and one without, and then two with and three without, etc., so that you are going back and forth between reinforced and not reinforced trials in a seemingly random manner. In this way, the presence of the reinforcer cannot be anticipated, just as with a slot machine. In this analogy, you are the slot machine and the dog is the gambler. This must be carried out very gradually, ensuring that the behavior does not deteriorate (i.e., extinguish), but in fact becomes stronger and more persistent. Don't prompt your gambler to go into rehab because he never seems to win—keep him on the hook and in the training game!

Training Tactic #8. Refine Form, Latency & Speed

Now that you have a behavior occurring reliably on cue and you do not need to reinforce every single occurrence of the behavior, you are in a good position to refine the behavior a bit, if needed.

Let's say that the form of the behavior is not great—it is reliable, but it looks a little off in the way the body moves. The form of the behavior will never be precisely the same each time it occurs; there will always be some small differences from instance to instance. You can actually shape a better form by selecting the variations of the behavior for reinforcement that are closer to what you ultimately want and failing to reinforce the not-so-close examples of it. One thing that happens when you fail to reinforce a behavior (as when you are thinning the schedule for instance) is that the form of the behavior becomes more variable. The dog might move a little faster, try a little harder, or move a bit differently. Within all the variations, some will look closer to what you ultimately want and some less so. While you were thinning the schedule, you were not using any criteria for which to reinforce and not, other than trying to make it seem random and gradually thinning. Now, you can pick and choose a bit. Try to stay close to the ratio of reinforcement you have been at, so that the behavior does not deteriorate, but expect just a little better form, and as soon as you get that, reinforce that one for sure. If the behavior is the same as before or "worse," fail to reinforce those occurrences. Once the form tends toward the better version pretty solidly, increase your expectation a little bit again and do the same thing. Do this until the form is as you want it. This is "shaping," one of the most powerful tools in training.

You might also find that the dog does not exhibit the behavior right away when the cue occurs, but instead, seems to get to it only after a few seconds. This timeframe between the cue and the behavior starting is called the "latency." You can reduce the latency with differential reinforcement, as discussed above for replacing problem behaviors. In this case, a long latency is the "problem behavior" and a shorter latency is the proper (criterion) behavior. Expect the behavior to initiated just a little bit sooner and reinforce those slightly sooner occurrences, failing to reinforce the behaviors that start later. Once the latency is reliably reduced a bit, you can up the expectation a little more and go through the process again, repeating the tactic until the behavior starts right away when the cue is delivered.

Finally, you might find that the behavior occurs rather slowly and you would like the motion of the behavior to occur a bit faster, a kind of response that might be characterized as enthusiastic. Handle this in same way you did for latency, selecting from the various slight differences in speed, reinforcing the quicker ones and failing to reinforce the slower ones until it meets the speed criterion that you have pre-established. Of course, this assumes you want the behavior to occur more quickly, which will not always be the case, and indeed you may carry out the same procedure to generate a slower behavior if you like.

Training Tactic #9. Proof Again Distraction, Duration, Distance & Diversity (The 4 Ds)

We discussed distraction, duration, distance, and diversity in a previous chapter and we revisit it here as a tactic for effective training. You want the behavior to occur in various places and under various kinds of distraction, for an appropriate duration, and you want the dog to exhibit the behavior even if you cue it when you are several meters away. Each of these parameters can be trained quite easily, if you follow the rules. The first rule is to work on one parameter at a time, from minimal expectation, up to your goal, keeping the other parameters at minimal expectation level. When you achieve success with one, relax the expectation for that one and work another parameter up separately. Only after two or more have been worked up to your goal, should you consider combining them in a gradually increasing manner again (this time, together).

Start training behaviors in a minimally distracting environment. Usually, that means starting in a boring room that does not have too many other things going on, including other animals or toys. Once the behavior is reliable in this environment, add a small amount of distraction. This might mean you move around a little bit while you cue the behavior or another person is present. You have to work at the pace of the conditioning. If you push too far with distraction, the behavior will not occur when cued and the training will deteriorate. Only when the behavior is reliable and smooth under the new distraction level should you introduce a slightly higher level of distraction. This can mean working up to having other people present who might otherwise distract/attract the dog. For instance, when training a dog to come to you when called, you might work up to having the dog interacting with someone else who is holding a toy and you call the dog away from them to you, reinforcing the appropriate behavior with a quick treat and release to go play with the other person and toy, which is now only available if they first come to you. You will likely see all of the principles and strategies playing out here. You may also work your way out of the boring room into more distracting rooms and eventually to a yard, and then eventually out onto a busy street or in a pet shop. Very gradually work on increasing the distraction level in the environment(s) in which you train.

Duration is not required for all behaviors. Duration, in this context, refers to the amount of the time the behavior is held in position (or sometimes repeated in rapid succession). For example, duration applies to sit or down, but not to a recall. Start by relaxing the distraction parameter back to minimal. Then, as with other components of training, start with a minimal duration (e.g., 1 second) before providing a treat. As soon as you provide the treat, the trial is over, so it is okay if the dog breaks position when you do so; it's just important that the position was maintained until you released them with a release cue or provided the treat. You are not fooling anyone, if you see them breaking positon and give the treat quickly as though to catch it in time—you did not. When they will remain in position for that second, breaking only once you release or offer the treat, start expecting two seconds, then three seconds, etc.

If the dog breaks position, remember the reactive strategies and the differential reinforcement procedure. Do not reinforce for that trial. Provide minimal stimulation, especially reinforcement, for a few to several seconds to avoid reinforcing inappropriate behaviors and then get back on track. Extinction trials such as these should be rare. If you start getting too many extinction trials (i.e., trials requiring reactive strategies), it means that you are increasing the duration element too quickly or by too large of an increment. Take it more slowly. Start to ping-pong the durations around a seemingly random average while very gradually increasing the duration requirement, until you have the behavior occurring for a reasonable amount of time.

Distance is important with some behaviors. Being able to cue a behavior when you are at a distance from the dog is important for behaviors like sit or for recall, but not for walking on loose leash. Distance training is important as a safety measure as well. If for some reason, your dog ends up on the other side a road, you want to be able to cue a solid sit that will be maintained for a duration long enough for you to get across the street to them. Distance is worked in a manner similar to how the other parameters were. Start by relaxing the other parameters and cueing the behavior up close. Very gradually increase your distance from the dog before you cue the behavior. Typically, you have to move excruciatingly slowly with increasing distance. You may need to tether the dog to something behind them or use a barricade but these preclusion procedures are best avoided if possible in favor of working very slowly and gradually.

Diversity refers to training the behavior in various locations, promoting generalization. You should start training a new behavior in one location for best results, but once the behavior is exhibited smoothly and reliably in that location, you can cue the behavior in a similar but different location. Gradually and incrementally, introduce new and different locations to cue the behavior to ensure the behavior ultimately generalizes to all of them.

You can combine two or all four of the parameters, but only once the ones you plan to combine are good and solid, and once the behavior is reliable at the expected criterion level. To combine parameters, start with all but one parameter relaxed (i.e., minimal). With the one parameter at the desired level, begin gradually reworking another parameter up from a low level. Once you have worked that one up, you should have both at high levels together and the behavior remains reliable. If adding a third parameter, relax that one and gradually work it up under higher levels of the other two. If this process is challenging, you may need to work that one up with just one of the others at high levels and then after that, working all four together.

Training Tactic #10. Maintain What You Have Achieved

Once you have a good solid, smooth and reliable behavior under all of the conditions described in previous tactics, you still need to maintain the behavior. You will need to ensure that the behavior is reinforced enough times that it does not deteriorate. If you find that it does start to deteriorate at some point, consider some refresher training. Make sure to cue the behavior in various environments on a regular basis to keep it reliable.

Enjoy the fruits of your, and your dog's, labor, each feeling they have effectively trained the other, you to get behaviors that make your life easier and them to get different kinds of reinforcers from you such as praise, treats, playing, walks, food etc.

Chapter 5. Behavioral Well-being Practices

Introduction

To this point, we have addressed mostly issues of training, including how to manage behavior in ways that support a mutually reinforcing social relationship between you and your dog. This is vital, given that you must live together, with the challenge of being from different species, and having different preferences and perspectives on life. However, much is shared in this regard between humans and dogs, providing a basis on which to share life. Understanding the basic principles of behavior, as well as understanding strategies and tactics for changing behavior, are key in achieving these goals. However, there is more to creating a mutually reinforcing relationship than becoming conditioned to change a dog's behavior to fall more in line with your expectations. This chapter is dedicated to this objective. Some of the practices described below overlap with one another. Some of the practices are geared toward promoting reinforcing interaction between you and your dog, while others are geared toward meeting the dog's basic behavioral and biological needs, which are prerequisites to establishing reinforcing social relationships.

Practice #1. Resolve Aversive Contingencies

This first practice involves identifying and resolving aversive contingencies. We come into contact with numerous aversive stimuli on a daily basis. Some of these stimuli are more readily escapable, or predictable (and hence avoidable), than others. Those that are not readily and quickly escapable/avoidable can generate incredibly resilient and unpleasant side-effects, particularly if they are intensely aversive.

Many aversive contingencies can be discontinued completely. If you have been utilizing aversive training practices or merely responding to certain annoying dog behaviors aversively, you can begin utilizing the content of this book in place of those practices, particularly the proactive strategies.

You may not be able to effectively generate a list of such practices, but you can resolve to recognize aversive contingencies when they occur and take note of them, reviewing the appropriate sections of this book and devising a new approach—ideally, a more proactive approach.

If the dog engages in a behavior that you find annoying and your usual reaction is to respond with aversive stimulation of one kind or another, recognize that the fact that the behavior persists means that this strategy has not been effective, that it is unpleasant, and likely generating problematic side-effects that you may not be aware of. Then, consider how you can address this differently. Consider what you might do *prior* to the behavior occurring to make that behavior less likely to occur to begin with.

If an annoying behavior nevertheless does occur, think about the consequences it generates; do not allow or contribute to reinforcing it as opposed to utilizing more aversive, and less productive, options. Even negative reactions might, in fact, be reinforcing the behavior. Consider what the dog is "getting out of it" and try to ensure that they can get that or something similar with less annoying behaviors.

As an example of aversive stimulation that can be merely discontinued, some dog owners use head halters to walk their dogs in order to keep the dogs from pulling on their leashes. In my experience, many, perhaps most, dogs respond poorly to these devices and never really come to tolerate them well. When the dog is wearing the head halter, the discomfort is not escapable. In addition, if the head halter is used inappropriately, it can potentially cause pain and possibly injury. Consider trying a standard body harness; with no specific training to the contrary, dogs generally tend to pull more when things are attached to their head/neck than when the leash is attached to the torso—the result of the "opposition reflex"—and/or engage in loose-leash training to eliminate the need for anti-pull devices. Other devices, such as choke chains and prong collars are even worse! Definitely avoid those as well as any shock devices, noise makers that are meant to interrupt or punish problem behaviors, things intended to be thrown at dogs, invisible fences, citronella spray collars, elastic muzzles to punish barking and so on, anything that generates aversive stimulation.

Some aversive contingencies cannot be avoided in this way. Some dogs react negatively to being left alone. This problem can be resolved, but it will require access to good information (such as O'Heare, 2016), and sometimes, a professional behavior technologist. Resolving this kind of problem will require time and energy as well. But it will eliminate a massive source of aversive stimulation and the fallout which that generates.

If the dog is harassed by either another pet or by children, a solution must be found. This might involve training the other pet or the child to leave the dog alone.

If pedestrians are causing the dog stress, consider blocking the view to them and/or providing white noise to prevent the dog from hearing other people. Remedial socialization may also be in order. If it is safe to do so, have strangers provide the dog treats.

Many dogs react poorly to visiting the veterinarian or having nails trimmed. In these cases, one may eliminate the aversive contingency by changing the emotional reactions and/or training behaviors that effectively avoid or escape them. Let's explore an example that will help elucidate the process for resolving problem emotional arousal, which can be applied to other problem situations.

If the dog responds problematically to having his or her nails trimmed, start with a tolerable level of stimulation-intensity and reinforce tolerant behaviors, moving on to reinforce slightly more intense contact with the stimulus only when the dog is tolerant of the first level of intensity and build on that success from there. This is one way to render an aversive contingency less or non-aversive.

For example, you might present the nail trimmers within sight of the dog and reinforce tolerant behaviors, repeating through several trials. Then, when the dog only exhibits tolerant behaviors (or even becomes excited when they see the nail trimmers because it has been paired with treats), hold the trimmers close to the dog's nail and reinforce tolerant behaviors again, repeating through several trials.

If, at any point, the dog becomes distressed in any way, exhibiting signs of stress or intolerant/escape behaviors, do not reinforce this, but more importantly, back up to a lower level of intensity of exposure and work your way up more slowly, ensuring success along the way.

Once the dog responds tolerantly to mere presence of the nail trimmer, briefly touch the nail with the trimmer and immediately reinforce for tolerant behaviors, repeating until the dog exhibits only tolerant behaviors in reaction to having their nail touched with the trimmer. Then, try trimming just one nail at a time for a little while before moving on to trim two at a time. Work your way up to being able to trim the dog's nails completely, while the dog exhibits only tolerant behaviors.

By taking this incremental (graded) approach, the dog's emotional reaction to nail trimming will change at the same time that you are reinforcing tolerant behaviors. *The environment is arranged such that a previously aversive contingency is rendered non-aversive and training without coercion can proceed.* Book two in the *Dog Behavior* series will provide more in-depth coverage of this process.

Practice #2. Promote Creativity, Persistence, and Resilience

Control is king! The "sense" of "being in control" is central what is commonly meant by the term "empowerment," and a lack thereof, is what is commonly meant by "disempowerment," a kind of conditioned helplessness that is a feature of so much behavioral torment for both dogs and humans. A "sense of being in control" is a belief of sorts, a verbal behavior exhibited by those who have experienced a history of effectively operating on their environment—that is, controlling the environment and generating added reinforcers and effectively escaping/avoiding aversers.

While a "sense of control" is of potential interest to natural scientists, these represent, at best, private behaviors only observable to a community of one—the person exhibiting that behavior. In behaviorology (and behavior analysis), such private contingencies are "externalized" and the emphasis is placed on behaviors that are observable and measurable by others. That is, we trace back through the causal chain until we arrive at an external cause for the behavior of concern that can more readily be manipulated in order to change the behavior. Since all behavior is fully caused, we know that something caused this belief behavior, and so, while the belief behavior is a real behavior, trying to deal with inaccessible causes is less productive than identifying and operating on the first available external cause. It also means operationalizing terms such as these, that is, reframing such terms in a way that allows us to work effectively with them. This topic can receive natural science attention so long as such nebulous terms are framed in natural science terms.

If "empowerment" is about the confidence generated by effective control over one's environment, then, in behaviorological terms, we are talking about "proficiency," or the generally higher degree of proficiency, referred to as "fluency" or "mastery." One is said to be proficient when their behavior, in relation to a specific task, is effective in generating reinforcement. A very effective repertoire is sometimes referred to as fluency or mastery.

Therefore, rather than discussing "empowerment" and "control" per se, our emphasis will be on conditioning for fluency, which means conditioning highly effective adaptive patterns of behavior (as opposed to specific discrete behaviors in this case). Specifically, certain behavioral "tendencies" or "patterns of behavior" tend to lead to an increased likelihood of contacting reinforcers. These general patterns of behavior or behavioral strategies can actually be reinforced like discrete behaviors are (see Pryor, 1969). In other words, we will discuss the training of some general behavior strategies that tend to benefit the subject in terms of accessing reinforcers and hence experiencing a greater degree of satisfaction in their lives. We will explore creativity, persistence, and resilience in turn.

"Creativity" refers to novel, yet productive, responding and is productive because where one behavior may not be effective, other behaviors may be. Rigid responding is rarely as successful a general strategy as creativity under appropriate circumstances, and a tendency to behave creatively in general, can be reinforced. A history of aversive stimulation often generates a tendency toward minimal and rigid responding, something that can be rehabilitated with the training described below.

"Persistence" refers to the tendency to persevere in responding in the face of blocked access to reinforcers (extinction and the resulting frustration it generates) rather than give up. Giving up at the first sign of blocked access is not usually a beneficial strategy in general since many reinforcers require specific forms of behavior, which may not have been initially exhibited. As you can see, this works in conjunction with creativity as well.

"Resilience" refers to what animal trainers commonly refer to as "bounce-back" after frustration, startle, or "fear." This is as opposed to falling apart, disengaging into helplessness, or becoming excessively and disruptively emotional. Just as creativity and persistence can be reinforced, so too can working *through* aversive events rather than shutting down or becoming excessively emotional.

Let us discuss the training of such tendencies, including rehabilitating "disempowerment."

Phase 1. As with any other form of training, the basic approach is to put the subject in a position to succeed in exhibiting the behavior of interest as opposed to other behaviors, and this even works when we put the subject in a position to succeed in exhibiting general patterns of behavior that function well to overcoming adversity. In other words, we start by ensuring a good solid history of success rather than failure and build from there.

This is achieved by arranging circumstances proactively, such that the subject is assured to operate effectively on the environment, generating reinforcement. This is particularly important for subjects with a history of aversive conditioning and resulting "disempowerment" (i.e., minimal and rigid responding).

A forthcoming book in the *Dog Behavior* series will address rehabilitation of such problems. If a dog has no such history and behaves in ways we might characterize as "confident," then it is fine to start directly into phase 2.

Phase 2. Once the subject begins responding in ways we might characterize as "confident," that is, they do not shy away from opportunities to earn reinforcers, we may gradually begin shaping greater creativity, persistence, and resilience in the face of adversity. This can be done serendipitously by recognizing instances of the dog persisting rather than quickly giving up, as well as exhibiting productive and variable behaviors, finding new ways to get reinforcers when access to reinforcers is blocked as opposed to behaving rigidly, and working through minor frustrations, startling events, or emotional reactions, rather than shutting down.

To achieve this, we must begin introducing *minor* impediments to reinforcement. These extinction trials will generate mild levels of frustration, which will generate an increase in behavioral variability and intensity of responding. Remember, life invariably involves at least mild frustrations, startling events, and the occasional problematic emotional reaction on a more or less regular basis—we cannot avoid all of them, and it is wise to prepare dogs (and children and others) to respond adaptively to these kinds of events! That is the kind of training in this section is designed for.

If the frustrations are arranged in a carefully graded manner, the subject will be in the best possible position to overcome the challenges effectively and they will exhibit even more "confidence"—they begin to demonstrating mastery over such events. In other words, we "prove to them" that they can indeed effectively overcome adversity. We build on this mastery by allowing common everyday frustrations, all the while, reinforcing any behaviors that might be considered creative, persistent, and resilient.

Over time, these general behavioral tendencies will generalize and be exhibited in reaction to other everyday challenges, allowing the subject to quickly and easily overcome many of them. It will also prepare the subject for the frustration of "not always getting what they want." There are after all, times when we cannot allow access to certain reinforcers, usually for the dog's own safety.

One of the ways we achieve this comes when you thin schedules of reinforcement during regular training. The dog experiences mild and temporary frustration at these times and may engage in any number of behaviors in reaction to that. If the schedule is thinned gradually, the dog will not likely fall to pieces and give up, but rather "try a little harder" or "try something else." Take these opportunities to reinforce this creativity, persistence, and resilience. This is a good start.

We can also achieve this training less serendipitously by manufacturing the occasion for such behaviors. One of the most powerful procedures for encouraging creativity, persistence, and resilience is shaping, something I will discuss further on in greater detail, but will introduce here as it relates to the current practice. Shaping is generally used in training behaviors that are not readily promptable in their final form and do not occur frequently enough to merely reinforce when they do occur. It involves identifying the terminal behavior and then reinforcing successive approximations to that "terminal behavior."

Start by generating and reinforcing an initial movement required for the terminal behavior, and when that is occurring reliably, expect a slightly closer approximation to the terminal behavior, and so on until the terminal behavior occurs.

Though not a technical term, "free-shaping," as it is called in animal training circles, involves shaping but with few or no prompts. The trainer merely waits patiently for the approximation among the variety of responses the subject will exhibit and reinforces it when it occurs. This requires more patience and some training skill from the trainer, but also requires more creativity, persistence, and resilience from the trainee. It is an advanced skillset that requires a high rate of reinforcement to avoid frustration, which means small approximations.

Whether one shapes with prompts or not, the minor frustrations involved when transitioning to expecting the next approximation (because the previous approximation is now under extinction) allows repeated opportunities for the dog to exhibit creativity, persistence, and resilience. These occurrences are then reinforced and become more prominent in the dog's general repertoire in other environments. This is how one trains such patterns of behavior.

One must, of course, be careful with such training. It is *vital* that, while we prepare the dog to handle the minor frustrations of everyday life adaptively, that we do *not* overdo it or move too quickly and cause the opposite effect.

The trick, in summary, is first to establish a strong history of success with minimal adversity, so that the dog is conditioned to be able to effectively contact reinforcement, and then condition the dog to react to the minor frustrations of everyday life with creativity, persistence, and resilience instead of excessive emotionality. This is achieved with a careful graded approach.

Practice #3. Enrich the Environment

Enrichment refers to manipulating the environment in such a way that provides the dog with an opportunity to exhibit species-typical behaviors and behavior patterns, resulting in contact with reinforcers associated with these kinds of behaviors. Enrichment causes minor beneficial stress (sometimes called "eustress," as opposed to "distress"). Without opportunities to exhibit species-typical behavior patterns, animals may resort to exhibiting "escape behaviors"—behaviors that function to reduce the distress caused by frustrated attempts to exhibit these behaviors and contact the reinforcers they generate. This might involve problematic behaviors that might evoke our saying the dog is "expending pent up energy." This might involve pestering, jumping up, excessive barking or other behaviors that people tend to find annoying. It might also result in behaviors that some people might refer to as "abnormal," such as stereotypical pacing or self-mutilation. These behaviors are not "abnormal"; they serve a perfectly explainable and normal function, which is to distract the animal from, or otherwise reduce, aversive feelings. It is perfectly "normal" to avoid or escape aversive stimulation. Enriching the environment just means providing the dog with opportunities to scavenge, hunt, play, engage in social behaviors etc. Let's explore a few ideas for environment enrichment.

Toys! Toys allow dogs to engage in a number of species-typical behaviors, including scavenging, hunting, and chewing. The first step is to identify the toys that are safe for your dog. My first dog could have unsupervised access to any kind of toy. He would never touch anything that was not his toy and he would never swallow any parts that he was able to pull apart or chew off. Since then, I have come to appreciate safety more, as I have dogs that will work quite hard to dismantle any toy and any part that comes off the toy and is big enough to swallow, will be swallowed. This has resulted in pain for the dog, very expensive vet bills (e.g., thousands of dollars for surgical removal), and very high stress levels for the dog and me. My dogs now only have access to very hard toys that they cannot dismantle or destroy. However, hard toys such as these can be a problem for some dogs, such as those dedicated chewers who will chew so hard that they break a tooth on the hard toy surface.

So, it is smart to get a selection of various safe toys for your dog. Consider rotating access to the toys, providing some for a few weeks, while the others are hidden away and then switch them out, perhaps with the exception of the dog's most favored toys. This will help keep things interesting for your dog. Hard plastic bone-shaped toy or Kong® toys are great for long-term chewing, while other toys require a different kind of interaction. For example, puzzle toys can be useful. Some are large balls or cubes, in which you place treats or food and the tidbits are released as the dog pushes the ball around. If you have a dog who eats too quickly, it can be fun to feed them their meals in these balls. Most are made of plastic though, so extra-special cleaning must be done to keep them clean and free from bacterial growth. Other toys, such as ball launchers that work in a manner similar to tennis practice machines, are great for dogs who like to play fetch. Other interactive toys release treats when the dog presses a button. These interactive, "thinking" toys allow the dog to be creative and are powerfully enriching.

Practice #4. Engage in Shaping and Sport Training

All appropriate training that utilizes non-coercive methods and maintains fun benefits the relationship between the dog and the trainer. But, some kinds of training tend to require more substantial participation by the dog, and often, interaction between the dog, the trainer, and the environment. You have become familiar with differential reinforcement in previous chapters. You have also become familiar with refining the form of behaviors. This is achieved with shaping, another topic that has been discussed above. I will review and extend our discussion of shaping here with an emphasis on the nuts and bolts of using the clicker because it is an advanced procedure that can benefit from reiteration in the context of the current practice.

Instead of just changing the rate of a behavior, shaping changes the form or "topography" of behavior. Shaping requires a more engagement and participation than some other simpler forms of differential reinforcement. But, if done well, it tends to promote creativity, persistence, and resilience, as discussed above.

Shaping is actually a series of differential reinforcement procedures carried out one right after the other. Shaping, as a means of changing, not just the rate of a behavior, but its form, is appropriate for training behaviors that the dog does not currently exhibit frequently enough to strengthen with simple added reinforcement and cannot easily be prompted in their final form. It may also be used for some behaviors that can be prompted in the final form, if you want to achieve them through the shaping process, specifically to get the benefits that only shaping provides.

For example, if you want a dog to spin in a circle, you could lure and easily reinforce for the desired movement. But, if you would like to engage in training that involves more empowering interaction between the dog and yourself, try shaping the behavior instead. Shaping breaks the behavior down into incremental approximations of the behavior and each one is trained in sequence. For example, if you want to train a dog to spin in a circle, you start with reinforcing a slight turn of the head in the correct direction and continue to reinforce this movement until it is occurring frequently. Then, set the criterion for a slightly greater turn of the head and reinforce *only* instances where the head turns *that* far, failing to reinforce the dog's head movements that don't meet that criterion.

Once you have that occurring frequently, increase the criterion again in a stepwise manner, until you are reinforcing turning completely around in a circle.

You may prompt behaviors to be shaped, but there is value in trying to avoid prompts as much as possible, by using what many trainers call "free shaping." In free shaping (i.e., without prompts), you simply wait for the desired behavior to occur without your help, then reinforce it. Prompts should be used if you and dog get stuck and frustration can be prevented with it. When free-shaping, it is particularly important to prevent frustration and one important way of doing that is to set very small approximations, ones small enough that you are reinforcing at least every 5 seconds.

It is a good idea to formalize your shaping plan in writing, so that you have something concrete to refer to during your training session. First, write down the behavior you ultimately want to achieve near the bottom of the page. This would be the "terminal behavior"—the final result that is achieved at the end of a list of incremental approximations. Then, identify the approximations that you will use to reinforce through the process. The approximations should be small enough that the normal variation in responding will mean that at least sometimes, you will get the approximation you need so that you can reinforce the behaviors and strengthen that before moving to the next approximation—at least every 5 seconds. Once you have your plan, gather your clicker (see below) and treats and start training.

You will likely see a number of fleeting behaviors that occur during shaping. These occur more so with shaping than is common in other procedures, an additional piece of equipment advisable. Treats reinforce behavior without any previous training. The problem is that in training where a lot of behaviors occur in rapid succession, by the time you provide the treat for a specific behavior, it is likely, and even certain, that a few other small-scale behaviors have occurred. This means that you actually reinforce the later behaviors, rather than the one that you wanted. Thus, it is very helpful to reinforce the precise, exact behavior that you wish to reinforce. This may not be possible with fleeting behaviors and so a "mark" is used to identify the exact behavior of concern, which is them followed by the treat. It is most helpful if you can mark that behavior in the split-second that it occurs. Furthermore, in some training sessions you may be too far away from the dog in order to provide treats to them in a reasonable timeframe. There needs to be some way to "bridge" the gap between the behavior and the reinforcement, because, as you know, reinforcement must be immediate and not delayed. Enter the "clicker." A clicker is a little handheld device that makes a click sound when you press a button. We use this as a "conditioned" reinforcer (in contrast to treats, which are examples of "*un*conditioned" reinforcers). But, a clicker does not reinforce behavior on its own or without conditioning to establish it—it must be trained as a reinforcer.

There are two ways of conditioning the clicker. Here is the first method: click the clicker and deliver a treat within two seconds, wait a few seconds and repeat. Repeat this sequence through several trials. Make sure to do this in different places and make sure that no particular behavior is occurring when you click and treat. After several trials, the click will have been biologically "paired" with the treats and the dog will come to react to it similarly to how they react to treats (emotionally) and that reaction functions as a reinforcer. This process is sometimes referred to as "loading" or "charging" the clicker. Some trainers begin charging the clicker as a stand-alone procedure as described above, but many trainers condition it (achieve the pairing) during the initial part of training a dog with no clicker experience. This is the second approach: begin training, prompting a behavior and then clicking and providing the treat as quickly as possible following the click, ideally within a second or so at first, and in this way, the clicker becomes a conditioned reinforcer as you begin your training. After several trials, you can extend the time between click and treat to 2 seconds.

The click only remains an effective reinforcer if it is at least occasionally and ideally continually, paired with the treats. So, it is good general rule to **always** follow every click with a treat within a couple seconds. The higher degree of contingency between the click and treat, the more effective the clicker will be as a reinforcer and it is a bad habit to let some clicks go without the follow up treat.

The clicker allows you to mark exactly the specific fleeting behavior you want to reinforce, even though other behaviors occur before and after the desired behavior. The clicker is only used in the beginning of training a new behavior or new feature of a behavior (like fine tuning the form of a behavior you have already trained). So, when training a new behavior, particularly in shaping projects, when the criterion behavior occurs (i.e., the one on your list you are currently working on meets the specific criteria for reinforcement), you click exactly just as the behavior is finishing, and then you provide the treat within a couple of seconds. You may click when the behavior reaches a "point of no return," so to speak, at first if the dog is likely to quickly engage in other behaviors immediately upon completing the behavior of concern. Then, transition to clicking just at the behavior is completed once you have strengthened that behavior a bit. If you're not close to the dog, this allows you time to walk in close or to toss the treats to the dog. That constitutes a single trial well done. You are then free to move on to another trial. The only difference is that you click the clicker exactly when you would ideally otherwise want to deliver the treat and then you follow the click up with the treat.

Back to shaping. Shaping is so powerful because it conditions the dog to exhibit general patterns of behavior that promote effective reactions to the environment in general and increase the dog's ability to contact reinforcers. It trains persistence as opposed to just giving up, creativity as opposed to rigidity, and resilience (i.e., the ability to "bounce back" after frustration/stress) as opposed to falling to pieces when frustrated (from extinction trials). These patterns of responding are adaptive and promote "empowerment" (i.e., a general "sense" of control) as discussed above.

Shaping can be used to achieve complex, useful behaviors, as well as fun tricks. In both cases, the training should always be fun! Modulate your expectations, so that you can work at a pace that is a little challenging for the dog, but results in the vast majority of trials being successful. You should be reinforcing every 5 seconds. If you're not reinforcing this often, you are expecting too much from the dog. Be enthusiastic and have fun yourself as well, marveling at how "smart" dogs are and how members of two completely different species can interact so effectively when utilizing the natural science of behavior principles and strategies. Make training sessions short, usually two to three minutes depending on the dog's interest and enthusiasm level. Always end your training sessions on a positive note. It can be very fun to design and implement small shaping projects. You will find that your dog will become quite familiar with how the process works and it gets easier. You should also start to notice the benefits and patterns of behavior described above after a little while. Enjoy the process!

Another kind of training that can make a good "bonding" experience is training for a specific human–dog sport. There are a great many options available, depending upon your interest, time, and physical capabilities. You can join clubs or take classes to help provide expert guidance and structure. If you're inclined, you can choose competitive or titling sports that also provide you with the reinforcement associated with such activities. Sports like flyball and agility are great, but there are numerous others out there. Find one that suits you and your dog (so long as the training emphasizes added reinforcement and fun). Most importantly, have fun!

Practice #5. Engage in Social Play

Play elicits emotional arousal (i.e., the elicitation of chemical secretions by glands and the persisting effect of the circulating chemicals) that are contrary to stress, anxiety, fear, panic, etc. Play can help to prevent or rehabilitate depression and helplessness, as well as boredom. Engaging in social play is a great way to have fun and build a mutually reinforcing relationship.

The most important tip for engaging in social play, is that it *must* be fun for the *dog*, as opposed to just being something *you* think *should* be fun. Many dog owners believe that rough play is fun for dogs but it is not nearly as often the case as many people think. A dog may participate because there is little choice, but it is often stressful for them. Yes, dogs engage in mock combat with one another. But, it is not always reinforcing in these cases either. Indeed, in some instances, it likely is fun for the dog. But, there is a problem, in that many dog owners ignore or are oblivious to indications of stress in dogs. This may result in a dog owner failing to recognize that their dog is experiencing stress. Because of this, they do not stop the rough play and the dog then endures an unpleasant experience. Therefore, it is generally better to avoid rough play in favor of other kinds of fun.

Fetch is great fun and also excellent exercise, as long as you utilize warm ups and cool downs and build up the cardiovascular endurance and muscular conditioning needed for strenuous exercise. Many dogs engage in fetch quite readily without any dedicated training. Be sure to reinforce bringing the ball back to you, usually by throwing it again right away. Fetch can be a bit monotonous. One practice I like, from AniEd Ireland (http://www.anied.ie, specifically from their Facebook page at https://www.facebook.com/aniedireland/) is to inject variety into games of fetch in order to increase stimulation/enrichment and also manage exercise intensity by playing a quick game of tug or cue a trained trick in between throws. Mix up the play sequences a bit, so they are unpredictable. This will increase attentiveness and make the play session much more fun.

Tug can be one of the best games to play with dogs as it involves a great deal of interaction between both parties. It is a form of fun that dogs are quite familiar with and is usually reinforcing. As with fetch, interject variety to make it a more interesting game or play session. Remember that any time teeth are involved, rules are needed in order to keep everyone safe. Here are the rules for tug:

1. Initiate games of tug contingent only upon appropriate/acceptable behaviors, and never following any problematic behaviors.
2. Only people, and never the dog, initiate games of tug, so that the dog does not initiate tug with children, or elderly people, or in any other inappropriate contexts.
3. Tug for no more than 5 seconds per bout and include no more than 6 bouts in any given session. Some flexibility is acceptable with this rule, depending on the dog's arousal level.
4. Say "Thank you" (or another release cue) to get the dog to release the toy at the end of each bout (use treats to prompt this at first and later just to reinforce it); continued play requires releasing when cued. Say "Take it" (or another cue) when the dog may take the toy again for a new bout.
5. Take at least a 5–second break between bouts. Maintain interest vocally or with a cue for another behavior that you can then reinforce with another bout of tugging.
6. Teeth never touch skin (even "accidentally"). If the dog's teeth touch your skin, say "Ouch," and ideally take the toy from the dog. If you don't take the toy, immediately release your hold on it and disengage, ending the game and social contact for at least several seconds. The dog can be conditioned to be careful and still have fun.

Chase games are fun as well, but generally, it is a good idea to be the one being chased as opposed to the one doing the chasing. You don't want your dog to get into the habit of running from you, as this could be quite hazardous if you ever need to get control of the dog quickly (e.g., if the dog is running toward traffic, etc.). Chase can also be interjected into other games and play sessions.

Practice #6. Provide Appropriate Exercise

As the old saying goes, "a tired dog is a good dog." Exercise not only expends energy that might otherwise go into "looking for trouble," but also establishes a beneficial physiological arousal that helps prevent problem behaviors (e.g., inappropriate digging, barking, escaping, destroying property, etc.).

How much exercise a particular dog needs depends on their breed, age and history of conditioning. While some dogs are satisfied with a brisk walk each day, others require more intense, daily, rhythmic, aerobic workouts to satisfy their need for physical activity.

In extreme cases involving excessively "fearful" or "anxious" dogs, exercise can be used to increase serotonin activity in the brain, promoting beneficial forms of arousal. Though this is not required for most dogs, a more intensive exercise program can benefit such dogs. Specifically, the exercise in these cases needs to be aerobic, predictable, and rhythmical exercise at moderate to high intensity, carried out regularly. Aerobic exercise involves vigorous exercise that encourages the heart and lungs to work harder, thereby decreasing the resting heart rate over time and increasing lung capacity. It requires use of the large muscles of the legs and back. It is different from strength training, which focuses primarily on building muscle mass and strength. Results from research on humans and rats suggest that some benefits may be experienced transiently after individual exercise sessions (perhaps due to endorphins), but more stable results may materialize after six weeks of moderate to intense exercise sessions, five days per week, for at least one hour each session (perhaps related to increases in serotonin activity). This is only a general recommendation. Dogs must be physically conditioned gradually for this kind of exercise regimen, and breeds will vary (often drastically) in what they can handle and what they require to sustain the appropriate benefits. For example, some terrier breeds may require more intense exercise, rather than moderate exercise. However, as indicated above, most dogs do not require extensive exercise programs to satisfy physical activity requirements.

The first step in designing an exercise program is to assess the dog. The dog should undergo a full veterinary evaluation to identify any structural or other medical issues that might affect how, when, and if, they should be exercised. Dogs require warm-ups and cool-downs in exercise sessions for the same reasons that humans do. Warm-ups dilate the blood vessels, increasing the supply of nutrients and oxygen to the muscles and nerve cells. They stretch the muscles, ligaments, and tendons, helping to prevent injury, and also help align bones and distribute joint fluids to the bone surfaces (Zink, 1997, p. 112). After exercise, a cool down period (e.g., a slow 5-minute walk immediately following exercise) can avoid problems associated with pooling of the blood, including dizziness.

The three primary variables in an exercise program are intensity, duration, and frequency. Some general principles to remember include:

- The duration of exercise should be inversely proportional to the intensity.

- During intense exercise sessions, take frequent play and rest breaks. Rest breaks should be similar to cool-downs, rather than being sudden stops in activity.

- Cross-training is an excellent way to keep the dog interested and engaged, and condition different muscle groups (e.g., swimming and fetch or jogging). This also helps prevent wear and tear on specific structures associated with repetitive movements.

- Always be observant for signs of fatigue, and adjust exercise intensity and rest breaks to manage/avoid the development fatigue. A dog who is frequently fatigued by intense exercise may begin to find exercise an aversive event. Look for:

  - lying down (often in the middle of a task) or remaining down when encouraged to do something;

  - excessive panting (perhaps with widening at the end of the tongue);

  - yawning;

  - general lack of enthusiasm or energy;

  - stumbling;

- anxiety, indicated by stressed facial expression (e.g., a wide grin with furrows under eyes and behind the mouth); and

- dragging feet when trotting (often you hear the nails scraping on the ground).

- Vary the intensity, duration, and, to a lesser extent, frequency of exercise to keep it stimulating. These aspects should be varied in an apparently random manner, but the averages should continue to increase gradually during conditioning. Once initial conditioning is complete, intensity, duration, and frequency should stay about the same, but perhaps one day could be moderate intensity for a longer duration and the next day could involve a shorter but more intense session. Amounts of exercise should not vary drastically but just enough to keep it exciting and prevent staleness.

- Try to vary the tasks and exercises within individual sessions, to help maintain enthusiasm and prevent staleness or injury.

- Provide access to water before, during, and after exercise, but avoid allowing the dog to gulp large quantities at once.

- Avoid exercising in very hot temperatures. On a hot day, reduce the intensity and duration of exercise, and observe the dog carefully for signs of fatigue. Take frequent rest breaks and try to be out of direct sunlight.

One final point to remember is that exercise is distinct from some other social activities such as a nice leisurely walk in the park, wherein the dog is allowed to meet other dogs and people, sniff fire hydrants and engage in other fun activities. Avoid replacing such activities with jogging or running outings that do not allow the dog to engage in reinforcing behaviors.

Conclusion

As you can see, many of the practices discussed in this chapter can be achieved simultaneously. Many training and play opportunities can involve exercise and stimulation. These will be your highest impact, most efficient practices, that should be fun for all involved and promote general "satisfaction."

Training Dogs

Chapter 6. Training Projects

In this chapter, we explore (a) a general set of stages and protocols for training any behavior, which you may apply to training anything; and (b) step-by-step instructions for training some common behaviors, which will reinforce your familiarity with the general stages and their application.

The primary thesis of this book has been understanding the basic principles and strategies so that you can derive your own set of step-by-step instructions to train any behavior. Another primary thesis has been that promoting mutually reinforcing relationships involves "training" at all times, as opposed to just training a few specific behaviors during a specific training "session." The instructions in this chapter provide examples of instructions deriving from basic principles, strategies, tactics, and practices. These examples will help you appreciate how the instructions are derived and make it easier for you to derive instructions for other behaviors. You should, of course, continue to appreciate that behavior is always occurring and so is training.

This chapter starts with a discussion of equipment and reviews how to "charge" the clicker. Then, the previous material in this book is used to provide a training plan to train a dog to sit. Instead of repeating the basic sequences for the rest of the behaviors in the chapter, the basic steps are emphasized and suggestions made for applying the principles, strategies, tactics, practices, and training stages to the specific behaviors in question. Pay particular attention to the first behavior, sit, as it will provide the most detail.

Equipment and "Charging" the Clicker

In most cases, equipment is minimal. I recommend a basic 6–foot nylon leash and standard nylon buckle collar, or better, a standard body harness for training outside. A clicker pouch (or chalk pouch that climbers use for chalk) can go on your waist behind your back. The treats should be soft, easy to chew, and pea-sized for a medium to large sized dog, smaller for smaller dogs, and should be something they can consume quickly.

The other piece of equipment you will need is a clicker. A clicker is a small hand-held box with a button that, when pressed, makes a "click-

click" sound. Once "charged" (conditioned), the click sound acts as a reinforcer. Recall that a behavior must be reinforced either during or immediately as the behavior is finishing. If you only use treats, you likely will not be able to time your delivery accurately enough. As briefly described in the previous chapter, to charge the clicker, simply click and then, within 2 seconds, deliver a treat to your dog. If you're right-handed, you may find it easiest to hold the clicker in your left hand, which will free up your right hand for luring and then delivering treats when you begin training behaviors. Repeat this sequence several times with several seconds between each trial. Ensure that no particular behavior is occurring when you click during this charging process and carry it out in a diverse set of environments. Always follow the click with the treat. After several trials, the click sound will come to elicit the same emotional reaction in your dog that the treat does, which means that the clicker will function as a reinforcer, as long as you continue to pair it with the treats. Remember, the click ends the behavior. That means that when the behavior occurs and you click, that means the dog is free to break whatever position they are in and move about. This can be handy, because it allows you another opportunity to cue the behavior again. Once you have achieved the initial charging of the clicker, you are ready to start using it in actual training. The other option is to charge the clicker as you train. In that case, simply begin training and deliver the treat as quickly as possible at first until the pairing has been achieved.

Another thing to note about using a clicker is that it is just used for the initial training of a behavior or component of one. Once the behavior is reliable and on a "thinning schedule of reinforcement" (i.e., you are not reinforcing each and every instance but reinforcing only some of them, gradually increasing the ratio of unreinforced and to reinforced trials), you can discontinue using the clicker and simply present treats, toys, or other interaction as the reinforcers. If, at any point, you train a new component, such as refining the form, latency, or speed of the behavior, you can use the clicker again, in order to ensure precise timing.

Common Training Projects

Each training project begins with a behavior objective. This will tell you exactly what you want to achieve. It will provide the cue, a detailed description of the behavior itself and a detailed description of the criteria you aim to meet in order to consider the project complete.

The word "latency" refers to the amount of time between your cue delivery and the beginning of the behavior. Usually, you want the dog to start the behavior fairly quickly, but occasionally a dog may begin longer after the cue than you prefer. In this case, you can reduce the latency to meet the criterion.

The word "duration" refers to the interval of time that the desired behavior is maintained. Duration is not applicable to all behaviors but it is to many. Usually, you will start requiring only minimal duration but you can gradually work it up to meet your criterion. The behavior, in such cases, should be maintained until you cue some other behavior to provide a release cue.

The term "relative frequency" refers to how many times, out of how many total opportunities to exhibit the behavior, the behavior was actually exhibited by the dog. For example, if you cue a behavior 10 times in a training session and the dog responded to criteria 5 of those times, then the frequency is 5 out of 10, or 50%. The key here is that for a behavior to be considered exhibited, it must meet the criteria that you are currently using. You also need to remember the "D-parameters" discussed previously.

As you read through the concise summaries, recognize the principles, strategies, tactics and practices being applied. This will help condition you to have greater proficiency in analyzing behaviors and in constructing your own training plans.

Sit

Training "sit" is important for many reasons, as it is used to control the movements of the dog under various situations and can make your life a bit easier. For example, the sit behavior keeps the dog positioned safely close to you when waiting for a traffic light to change, it prevents the dog from interfering with others who may not be as into dogs as you are, it allows you to get food bowls to the ground without the irritating interference of the dog pushing to get the food, it allows you to get doors open without the dog rushing out or getting jammed up as you try to get the door open, and it allows you to greet the dog without them jumping up all over you, and so on. Indeed, a reliable sit provides many advantages in the interactions between the dog, owner, and environment.

Let's start with a formal behavior objective:

Behavior Objective

Cue: "Sit."

Behavior: Contact rear end to the ground (or as close as is physically possible) with front paws on ground, front legs straight and front paws within 5 inches of back paws.

Consequence: Treats and continued social interaction.

Criteria: Latency: 2 sec.; duration: until released, minimum 1 min.; relative frequency: 100% through 10 trials; distance: minimum 6 meters; distraction: various (e.g., other people and dogs present, reinforcers present); diversity: different rooms, back yard, sidewalks, in pet shops.

Preliminaries

Motivating operations & equipment. Start when the dog is hungry and not overly excited or too tired. Begin in a minimally distracting room. Have treats in a treat-pouch, ideally attached to your belt behind your back.

Acquisition Stage

Prompt and reinforce the behavior. To prompt sitting, place a small treat between your thumb and fingers. Ensure you have a good grip on the treat, so that the dog cannot grab it before you let it go. With your palm facing up, allow the dog to sniff the treat. Move it around to ensure the dog is "targeting" it, that is, that the dog's nose goes where the treat goes. Once the dog is targeting the treat, move the treat slowly over their head so that they crane their neck to continue targeting it.

If they jump up to target the treat, it is likely that you are holding the treat too far above their head. In that case, retract the treat, wait for a few seconds, contributing as little stimulation of any kind to the situation to reset to try again, this time with an adjusted movement that will not promote jumping.

If the dog shuffles back instead of sitting, do the same thing. You might then want to perform the targeting with the dog's rear end close to a wall or corner so that they are unable to back up (just be careful that the dog does not "feel cornered").

As the dog cranes his or her neck to target the treat, he or she should sit. You now have a trial that meets your training criteria. Once the dog has exhibited the target behavior, immediately click and deliver the treat to the dog, smile, and tell them how awesome they are. We often refer to this as merely "click and treat." Clicking released the dog and giving the treat ends the trial. Therefore, if the dog gets up after the click, that is fine; if the dog remains standing, you're set to repeat the trial. Carry out a few more trials. You should be able to perform the luring motion more quickly and effortlessly in each successive trial, as the prompt and other stimuli take on stronger control over the behavior.

Manage pace, enthusiasm, and rate of reinforcement. Set the criteria in all of the parameters to be trained as you continue to train to ensure success in the vast majority of, if not all, trials, meaning that reinforcement should be delivered at least about every 5 seconds, but maintain a degree of difficulty that promotes the dog's interest and progress. This judgment in maintaining smooth progress and minimal frustration is the trickiest set of trainer skills to teach people and the most challenging skill to acquire, primarily because it requires the use of many related training practices to be carried out reliably and quickly. Remain enthusiastic and have fun with your dog as you train.

Fluency Stage

Fade food-in-hands. After the first few trials, begin fading the food component of the prompt. Start with a few rapid trials of the sequence with the treat in your hand. Then, in the next trial, leave the treat in your treat pouch, and perform the prompt motion just as before. The momentum, the similarity of the trials, and remaining odor of the treat in your hand will help generate the behavior. Once exhibited, click and treat (i.e., reinforce). Through the next several trials, continue to reinforce on a continuous reinforcement schedule (i.e., click and treat for each sitting behavior). In most cases, you can simply fade the treat-in-hand stimulus permanently this way.

If the dog seems "apprehensive" with this change, you can fade the prompt more gradually. In this case, carry out the first trial without the treat in your hand as above and reinforce. Then carry out another trial, this time with the food in your hand. Through the next several trials, alternate between having the treat in your hand and not, in a seemingly random manner, gradually increasing the ratio of food-out-of-hand to food-in-hand prompts until you can run through several trials without the treat in your hand, and the dog smoothly exhibits the behavior.

Manage session features. Always end your training sessions on a positive note. If you believe that the dog is becoming satiated (i.e., full and "bored") with the reinforcer, restless, or it appears that the training may soon slowdown in terms of progress, end the session. If things are not going as well as you would like, end the training session by cueing a behavior that the dog already exhibits fluently, reinforce the behavior and work on the new behavior later. If you believe the dog can continue without deterioration of the training, then continue, but always strive to end sessions before deterioration of any component begins. Most training sessions should only be about 2 to 5 minutes. If you are not clicking and treating at least every 5 seconds, you are pushing too fast or expecting too much from the dog.

Establish a temporary cue. To start your next session, briefly review the training from the previous session, to ensure a reliable start to training. There are a few new protocols to execute at this stage of training. You should now be presenting the prompt without food in your hand at all. The luring motion should be taking control of the behavior at this point. Before this becomes too well established, begin fading the prompt, transferring control from the lure motion to a hand signal.

One common hand signal used for "sit" is a palm up motion from a straight arm to an articulated arm, either all the way or just half way, while you stand straight up. This resembles the lure motion, so transferring stimulus control is an easy process in this case. Make the current stimulus (the lure motion) seem (in this case, look) increasingly like the new stimulus (the hand signal) during each successive trial over several trials. Do this incrementally and gradually, and the dog should continue to exhibit the behavior reliably through each trial. If not, you are probably moving too quickly through this process.

You should now be able to evoke the behavior with the hand signal alone every time. Use this temporary cue until the behavior is fully formed the way you want it.

Introduce a release cue. It's now time to introduce a release cue. Now that you are not reinforcing every single trial with a treat, it is difficult to establish the end of a trial when not every trial ends with treat delivery. This also allows you to work on increasing the duration of the behavior more easily. You can use "you're free" as the release phrase or pick something else, but try to avoid phrases that are common in everyday discourse such as "thank you" or "okay." You can introduce the release stimulus as you train.

Begin presenting the release stimulus right before you click. If the dog does not break position when released, you can prompt it easily enough with open arms, backing up and praising the dog, or offering the treat at a slight distance, requiring the dog to break position in order to eat the treat. This is useful because then the dog is not still sitting when you want to try another trial.

Thin the schedule of reinforcement. Until this point, the behavior has been on a continuous schedule of added reinforcement. You can now move to a gradually "thinning" intermittent schedule, specifically, what we call a "variable ratio schedule." Some, but not all, criterion behaviors are reinforced in a variable and seemingly random manner like a slot machine. The goal here is to gradually thin the schedule of reinforcement in an indiscernible pattern. Start by failing to reinforce a response, but quickly carry out another trial and reinforce that one. Now, gradually increase the ratio of unreinforced trials to reinforced trials around a gradually increasing average. Randomize reinforced and unreinforced trials in a ping-pong manner, to avoid producing discernible patterns.

Beware of "ratio strain," wherein the schedule is thinned too quickly, the dog becomes frustrated, and the behavior becomes unreliable or unstable, and can actually extinguish. Be sure to always progress at the dog's pace.

Refine form, latency, and speed. Once you have begun thinning the reinforcement schedule, you may begin refining the form, latency, and speed. Determine if any of these features do not meet your criteria stated in your behavior objective. Work on only one of these features at a time. In working form, identify which motion needs changing. Extinction (the trials you don't reinforce) will increase variability in responding, so start reinforcing the behaviors that are closer to or meet your intended changed criterion and do not reinforce the others. Once the form is improved to criterion, you can work one of the other factors. Continue to require your chosen form changes.

If the dog does not begin exhibiting the behavior quickly enough after the cue, begin reinforcing the behaviors that begin more quickly and do not reinforce the ones that do not.

Work speed in the same manner. Reinforce the quick behaviors and not the slow ones until the dog meets the selected criteria.

Establish permanent cue. Once you have the behavior's form and latency established to your criteria, you should establish the permanent vocal cue. To transfer control from the hand signal to the vocal cue, simply repeat the sequence of *new* stimulus (vocal "sit"), followed by the *old* cue (hand signal), followed by occurrence of the behavior, followed by reinforcement. Achieve several trials and the new stimulus should take on control of the behavior. Pause after saying, "sit," to determine whether the dog will sit in response to just the vocal cue. It might take an extra second or two, as the dog waits for the hand signal, but they will likely exhibit the behavior. If not, repeat several more trials and try again until the new vocal cue evokes the behavior on its own.

Proof against the D-parameters: Distraction, distance, duration & diversity. Now that the behavior is under stimulus control, it is time to begin "proofing" the behavior against dynamic real-world challenges involving the four D-parameters. Remember to work only one at a time. Unlike refining form, latency, and speed, when you work another D-parameter, you relax the expectation for the others you have already worked. With form, latency, and speed, once you achieve your criterion, you maintain that expectation.

Start by introducing small distractions such as a motionless and quiet person positioned nearby, but looking away from the dog. Take the schedule of reinforcement briefly back to continuous reinforcement and gradually thin it with the new D-parameter in place. Introduce incrementally greater magnitude versions of the distraction, but again, do this at a pace that maintains the reliability of the behavior. Get a good start on distraction, and then when you work another D-parameter, relax distraction until you increase the other D-parameter. Then you can start combining them.

Distance involves and requires duration—therefore, it is best to work on duration before introducing distance. Train duration in the same way as you did distraction. Set a specific criterion and establish it reliably before increasing it again. Up to now, you have been reinforcing the sit immediately upon the dog's exhibiting the sit behavior. So, begin to require the dog to stay in the sit position for at least two seconds before reinforcing. Move at the dog's pace to ensure that almost all of the trials meet the duration criterion.

If you see the dog is just about to get up, resist the temptation to release and/or treat in order to avoid the non-criterion trial. You did *not* catch it in time. Releasing or giving a treat to the dog at this point will only result in reinforcing the behavior of getting up. When the behavior fails to meet the duration criterion, wait several seconds, contributing as little stimulation of any kind to the situation, identify the reason for your failure in generating the behavior (you likely waited too long or allowed excess distraction), reset, and try again.

In the case of distance, you should be able to simply inch your way further from the dog through successive trials. Work this D-parameter up gradually as with the others, and once it is well on its way, you can begin combining D-parameters. When you combine more than one D-parameter, remember to gradually build them up again.

For diversity of environments, instead of training in your living room, try several trials in the kitchen. Remember to relax other D-parameters briefly, return to a continuous schedule of reinforcement and then re-thin the schedule. This can usually be done quickly, but always minimize the level of the dog's frustration and stress, and keep your training fun. Then, select another area in which to train (e.g., a boring backyard, perhaps after already being out for a while to promote satiation with regard to the other reinforcers in the yard). Then, move locations and repeat the process at each new location. You may want to start in your front yard, move to the sidewalk, go down the street a bit and so on. Make sure to take the opportunity to reinforce occurrence of the behavior in many different places and under many different circumstances outside of formal training sessions.

Maintenance Stage

Continue to expand proficiency. Once you have achieved the final form, speed, and latency criteria of the target behavior, it is under control of a permanent cue, and reliably proofed through the D-parameters, it's time to begin working toward maintenance. You will likely want to continue to develop proficiency in new locations or with new distractors, but once you are well along into the process, it is time to begin transitioning from the intensive training activities of the fluency stage to less intensive maintenance of the fluency you have achieved.

Generalize reinforcers. Begin generalizing the reinforcers from just treats, for instance, to praise some times, and petting, or perhaps a quick game of tug, as long as the other activities are actually reinforcing.

Begin using fewer trainer-provided reinforcers, too. Use every-day reinforcers in order to help you maintain control over the behavior. For example, if eating is reinforcing, then take the opportunity to require a sit before allowing the dog access to their food. If going outside or having a leash put on acts as a reinforcer, require a sit while you open the door or prepare the leash. The same goes for sniffing fire hydrants or meeting other dogs and so on.

If at any point, any component of the training seems to be deteriorating, refresh the training by building that parameter back up.

Down

Down is a very useful behavior, as it allows you to encourage a dog to settle down and take a break. However, it is important to note that the down position can make many dogs feel "vulnerable," so you may want to avoid using it when strangers are around, when you are in public, or in any other situation that will make lying down aversive. Here is a behavior objective:

Behavior Objective

Cue: "Down."

Behavior: Contact both elbows, and either both hocks or either hip, with the ground.

Consequence: Treats and continued social contact.

Criteria: Latency: 2 sec.; duration: until released, minimum 3 min.; relative frequency: 100% through 10 trials; distance: minimum 6 meters; distraction: various (e.g., various reinforcers/distractions being present); diversity: different rooms and back yard.

Preliminaries

Motivating operations & equipment. Start when the dog is hungry, and not over-excited or too tired. Begin in a minimally distracting room. Have treats in a treat-pouch, ideally attached to your belt.

Acquisition Stage

Prompt and reinforce the behavior. The prompt for down involves holding the treat in your fingers with your palm facing downward, moving the treat directly down from the dog's nose, toward the floor between their feet. Click and treat when the behavior occurs and repeat until it is reliable.

Fluency Stage

Fade food-in-hands. Begin fading the food component of the prompt as was done for sit.

Manage session features. End sessions on a positive note. Use pace and enthusiasm, as well as a high rate of reinforcement (at least every 5 seconds) to ensure the dog's participation.

Establish a temporary cue. Establish a temporary cue by gradually making the lure motion look more like a hand signal. One hand signal for down is maintaining your elbow at your side, with your hand, palm faced downward, straight out in front of you and straightening the arm so that it goes down to your side. It is similar to the hand signal for sit, except that the movement is down toward the ground, rather than up and your palm faces downward rather than up.

Introduce a release cue. Begin presenting a release cue (e.g., "you're free") right before you click. Encourage the dog to break position at that point by where you deliver the treat.

Thin the schedule of reinforcement. Begin gradually thinning the reinforcement schedule with no discernable pattern. You will go back to continuous reinforcement any time you increase the level of difficulty or introduce a new feature, and then gradually re-thin the schedule again.

Refine form, latency, and speed. Compare the dog's average performance against your criteria for form, latency, and speed. Where necessary, refine each, one at a time, by gradually expecting a little closer of an approximation toward your goal (i.e., criterion). Maintain the expectation for any refinements made when you move on to work another (i.e., don't relax the criterion for what you have improved).

Establish permanent cue. To transfer control from the hand signal to the vocal cue, simply repeat the sequence of new stimulus (vocal "down"), followed by the old cue (hand signal), followed by occurrence of the behavior, followed by reinforcement, and repeat this sequence through several trials. The new cue will eventually take on control over the behavior.

Proof against the D-parameters. Begin proofing the behavior against distraction, duration, distance, and diversity of environments, one at a time, relaxing the criteria for others when working one of them. Once each reaches criterion, they may gradually be combined.

Maintenance Stage

Continue to expand proficiency. Ensure you continue to use the cue and behavior on a regular basis in diverse environments, and to maintain or refine their features.

Generalize reinforcers. Begin using varied reinforcers, including games and toys, as well as everyday reinforcers like eating, going outside, meeting others, and investigating interesting things.

Wait

"Wait" can be useful at doors, when being fed, before grabbing a toy, or in any circumstance where you would like the dog to briefly halt their movement. Wait is not used to have a dog stay in a position they have been cued to be in, such as sit or down. "Stay" or "wait" are not necessary in these cases, because the training requires the dog to remain in the position they have been cued to be in until released. Wait is used when no duration-relevant behavior has been cued before it.

Behavior Objective

Cue: "Wait."

Behavior: Cease moving if in motion and remain motionless otherwise.

Consequence: Treats and continued social contact.

Criteria: Latency: 0.5 sec.; duration: until released, minimum 1min.; relative frequency: 100% through 10 trials; distance: minimum 6 meters; distraction: various (e.g., various reinforcers/distractions being present such as doors being opened, toys or food being presented, etc.); diversity: different rooms, back yard, streets, pet shop.

Preliminaries

Motivating operations & equipment. Start when the dog is hungry and satiated with respect to the first reinforcer you apply to the behavior. Begin in a minimally distracting room. Have treats in a treat-pouch, ideally attached to your belt.

Acquisition Stage

Prompt and reinforce the behavior. In the case of wait, you can place your hand in front of the dog's face like a stop signal, which will likely engage the dog's attention, which in turn, will cause a brief hold on the dog's position. Begin by reinforcing after a 1–second hold and repeat through several trials.

Fluency Stage

Fade food-in-hands. Begin fading the food component of the prompt as was done for sit.

Manage session features. End sessions on a positive note.

Establish a temporary cue. In the case of wait, the stop signal hand motion acts as the temporary cue.

Introduce a release cue. Begin presenting a release cue (e.g., "you're free") right before you click. Encourage the dog to break position at that point by where you deliver the treat.

Thin the schedule of reinforcement. Begin gradually thinning the reinforcement schedule with no discernable pattern. You will go back to continuous reinforcement any time you increase the level of difficulty or introduce a new feature, and then gradually re-thin the schedule again.

Refine form, latency, and speed. Compare the dog's average performance against your criteria for form, latency, and speed. Where necessary, refine them, one at a time, by gradually expecting a little closer of an approximation toward your goal (i.e., criterion). Maintain the expectation for any refinements made when you move on to work another (i.e., don't relax the criterion for what you have improved as you would with the D-parameters).

Establish permanent cue. To transfer control from the stop signal hand motion to the vocal cue, simply repeat the sequence of new stimulus (vocal "wait"), followed by the old cue (stop signal hand motion), followed by occurrence of the behavior, followed by reinforcement and repeat through several trials. The new cue will eventually take on control over the behavior.

Proof against the D-parameters. Begin proofing the behavior against distraction, duration, distance, and diversity of environments, one at a time, relaxing the criteria for others when working one of them (unlike with form, latency, and speed). Once each is to criterion on its own, they may gradually be combined.

Maintenance Stage

Continue to expand proficiency. Ensure you continue to use the cue and behavior on a regular basis in diverse environments, and to maintain or refine their features.

Generalize reinforcers. Begin using varied reinforcers, including games and toys, as well as everyday reinforcers like eating, going outside, meeting others, and investigating interesting things.

Coming When Called (Recall)

Coming when called is of vital importance for safety! This particular behavior must be reliable under *highly* distracting conditions, so it is particularly important to train for high levels of distraction. Another important feature of training a solid recall is that it cannot just be trained in scheduled training sessions; it must be supported by adhering to certain rules *at all times*, which will be elaborated below.

Behavior Objective

Cue: "Here."

Behavior: Approach caller.

Consequence: Treats and continued social contact.

Criteria: Latency: 2 sec.; speed: at least a trotting gait; relative frequency: 100% through 10 trials; distance: minimum 12 meters; distraction: various (e.g., interacting with other dogs, other people, from couch and bed, away from objects like fire hydrants); diversity: different rooms, back yard, dog park, streets.

Preliminaries

Motivating operations & equipment. Rule 1. Avoid calling a dog when coming to you will end the fun (e.g., playing with other dogs) or to start something unpleasant (e.g., nail trimming). *Rule 2*. Reinforce as much as possible, every time your dog comes to you, whether you cued the behavior or not. Coming to you *must* be reinforcing for the dog in order for the behavior to be effectively put on cue. This means that you have to manage the dog's behavior carefully, think and plan proactively, and ensure you follow the rules.

Start when the dog is hungry and not overly excited or too tired. Begin in a minimally distracting room. Have treats in a treat-pouch, ideally attached to your belt behind your back.

Acquisition Stage

Prompt and reinforce the behavior. One way to arrange to generate the opportunity to prompt and reinforce the behavior is to have two people positioned a few meters apart at first, one (the distractor) holding the attention of the dog in a minimally distracting manner at first in a minimally distracting room. The other person (the trainer) engages in prompt behaviors that are likely to get the dog to come to them, including crouching down with open arms, making attractive noises (avoid the word "here" for now, unless you know for sure the dog will come to you). If you need to use treats to lure the behavior do so, but if it turns out to be unnecessary, that's better, as they would need to be faded later. If this proves too distracting, have the other person turn and look away when the cue is delivered in order to reduce the level of distraction further.

Fluency Stage

Fade food-in-hands. If food prompts were necessary, begin fading the food component of the prompt.

Manage session features. End sessions on a positive note. Use pace and enthusiasm as well as a high rate of reinforcement to ensure the dog's participation.

Establish a temporary cue. If you're very sure that the dog will come to you when you vocalize, you can simply begin using the permanent cue right away. However, this is not always effective. In many cases, you will need to use some motions and vocalizations together. As soon as practicable, begin fading out unnecessary prompts, leaving only the minimal amount of prompting that will get the dog to come to you. This involves making motions gradually less prominent and vocalizations gradually quieter and/or shorter. If this allows you to end up with just the permanent cue, great, but if it leaves you with a simpler prompt package, that is also fine, at this point in the training.

Introduce a release cue. Begin presenting a release cue (e.g., "you're free") right before you click. In the case of coming when called, this might be after the dog has come to you and pays attention to you for a couple of seconds, until released. Encourage the dog to break position and then deliver the treat.

Thin the schedule of reinforcement. Begin gradually thinning the reinforcement schedule with no discernable pattern. You will go back to continuous reinforcement any time you increase the level of difficulty or introduce a new feature, and then gradually re-thin the schedule again. For coming when called, it is good to maintain a somewhat rich schedule of reinforcement. Always provide praise and usually provide treats, play, or if (and only if—don't assume) reinforcing, physical contact.

Refine form, latency, and speed. Where necessary, refine each, one at a time, by gradually expecting a little closer approximation, moving toward your goal (i.e., criterion). Maintain the same expectation for any refinements previously made when you move on to work another (i.e., don't relax the criterion for what you have improved as you would with the D-parameters).

Establish permanent cue. If you have not established a permanent cue for coming when called, then at this stage the behavior should be reliable and you may do so establish one. Deliver the permanent vocal cue "here," provide the prompt, and reinforce the behavior when it occurs. After several trials, you will be able to drop the prompts and the vocal cue should evoke the behavior itself.

Proof against the D-parameters. Begin proofing the behavior against distraction, duration, distance, and diversity of environments, one at a time, relaxing the criteria for others when working one of them. Once each is exhibited to criterion on its own, they may gradually be combined.

As training progresses, the level of distraction can be increased (e.g., having the "distraction person" interacting in a more animated manner with the dog, or holding a toy or treats). Proceed slowly though, and increase distraction only when the dog's behavior at the level you are working on is reliable. This can be done outside later, and eventually, you can work up to calling the dog away from other people, dogs, or things they are engaged with, including highly effective reinforcing things (e.g., a favorite person or dog friend). Until the training is solidly reliable, when you call a dog away from their interaction with a reinforcer, the best reinforcer is allowing just a quick check-in and release. In other words, once they have arrived, click and treat or release them to go back to their interaction with the reinforcer.

Maintenance Stage

Continue to expand proficiency. Ensure you continue to use the cues and behavior on a regular basis in diverse environments, and to maintain or refine their features.

Generalize reinforcers. Begin using varied reinforcers, including games and toys as well as everyday reinforcers like eating, going outside, meeting others, and investigating interesting things.

Special note

You may wish to train the dog to sit automatically when they reach you, and to allow you to put a leash on them. To do this, cue the sit once the dog arrives, and click and treat. Repeat consistently and after several trials, delay cuing the sit to determine if coming to you has taken on control over the behavior. In other words, you cue "here" and the dog comes to you, you wait to see if the sit occurs without another interjected cue. If it does, click and treat. If not, do several more trials before testing again until coming to you and sitting upon arrival occurs together with just the one "here" cue.

You may also require the dog to wait tolerantly while you put the leash on. Do this once sit is well established.

Take It / Drop it

"Drop it" and "take it" are useful because they allow you to quickly get potentially dangerous things away from the dog. This also provides a good basis for training the dog to retrieve, which can be fun and provide great exercise. It can also be used to train the retrieve and drop it cues necessary in some obedience trials (e.g., retrieval of gloves and dumbbells). It is helpful to train "take it" and "drop it" together, since exhibiting one provides a perfect opportunity to exhibit the other and because "take it" is usually an effective reinforcer for "drop it." However, remember that it is usually best to train behaviors individually, rather than blending the training.

Behavior Objective

Cue: "Take it."
Behavior: Take and hold an object in the mouth.
Consequence: Toy or another item, but eventually, opportunity "Drop it" and its associated reinforcement.
Criteria: Latency: 2 sec.; duration (held in mouth): 20 sec., minimum 10 sec.; relative frequency: 100% through 10 trials; distraction: various (e.g., taken object minimally reinforcing, highly effective reinforcers present, other people, other dogs); diversity: different rooms, back yard, streets, pet shop.

Behavior Objective

Cue: "Drop it."

Behavior: Release from the mouth whatever is in it.

Consequence: Treats and continued social contact.

Criteria: Latency: 1 sec.; relative frequency: 100% through 10 trials; distance: minimum 6 meters; distraction: various (e.g., highly effective reinforcers taken and otherwise present, other people, other dogs); diversity: different rooms, back yard, streets, pet shop.

Preliminaries

Motivating operations & equipment. Start when the dog is hungry and satiated with respect to the first reinforcer to which you plan to apply the behavior. Begin in a minimally distracting room. Have treats in a treat-pouch, ideally attached to your belt in the back. Prepare a list of all the most effective reinforcer toys for the dog. Start with the *least* effective item, and if need be, ensure satiation.

Acquisition Stage

Prompt and reinforce the behavior. For training techniques like this one that are difficult to train with only two hands, it is usually most effective to hold the toy with one hand, and the treat and clicker in the other hand. Hold the treat between the index finger, middle finger, and thumb. Keep the clicker in the palm of the treat hand, with the button available to the small or third finger. You could hold the toy and clicker in one hand, but the clicker will likely be too close to the dog's ear (the clicking sound might startle them).

Hold the item, and encourage the dog to chew on the other end of it. Keep hold of the item! Once the dog has it in his or her mouth, wait a few seconds, say "drop it," and then hold up a very tasty treat. The dog will usually let go of the item to investigate the treat, especially if you started with a minimally reinforcing toy for them to hold onto and a relatively effective reinforcer to trade for it. As soon as they open their mouth and release the item, click, deliver the treat, and offer them the item back while you are still holding onto it. If you are confident that the dog will take the item back, say "take it" after you present it to them, but before they actually take it.

Begin testing the effectiveness of the "take it" cue by waiting for a few seconds before presenting the cue. If the dog mouths at the item before you present the evocative stimulus, gently retract the item, otherwise contributing as little stimulation to the event as possible for several seconds to reset the environment and repeat, offering the opportunity to wait for the item again. Once the dog waits for the cue before attempting to take the item, click and give the item to the dog.

Fluency Stage

Fade food-in-hands. Repeat the sequence several more times, and then quickly attempt a trial without the treat in your hand. Repeat the sequence several more times with no treats in your fingers but maintain continuous reinforcement.

Manage session features. End sessions on a positive note. Use pace and enthusiasm, as well as a high rate of reinforcement to ensure the dog's participation.

Establish a temporary cue. In most cases, you will not need a temporary cue for these behaviors and you can begin using the permanent cue right from the beginning. This assumes the dog will reliably let go of and take the item.

Introduce a release cue. You will not require a release cue for drop it, but you can establish one for these behaviors. You may install a release cue for take it, or you may simply work up to the 20–second criterion and leave it at that.

Thin the schedule of reinforcement. Begin gradually thinning the reinforcement schedule with no discernable pattern. You will go back to continuous reinforcement any time you increase the level of difficulty or introduce a new feature, and then gradually re-thin the schedule again.

Refine form, latency, and speed. Where necessary, refine your criteria, one at a time, by gradually expecting a little closer of an approximation toward your criterion. Maintain the expectation for any refinements made when you move on to work another (i.e., don't relax the criterion for what you have improved as you would with the D-parameters).

Establish permanent cue. In most cases, you will have established the permanent cue for these behaviors right from the beginning.

Proof against the D-parameters. Run through this protocol with the next item on the list of most effective reinforcers. Work your way through each of the items on the list in this manner.

Start to practice relinquishing contact with items that the dog has already had contact with for some time, as well.

You may wish to allow the dog to simply drop the item to the floor rather than into your hands sometimes, so that you can pick it up and offer it back to them.

Occasionally, practice not offering the item back to the dog. In this case, provide several treats that will take the dog a few seconds to find on the floor and eat while you place the item out of sight. It is important that you condition the dog such that the item will sometimes not come back. The distraction and the highly effective nature of the treats will help maintain the behavior under this condition.

Once you have worked your way through most of the dog's favorite toys, begin practicing trials with other items outside of training sessions. Part of what controls the behavior is the context of a training session arrangement.

Practice presenting the cue with these items at seemingly random times, as well as when the dog is already in contact with the items, without you having encouraged the dog to take it first.

Begin proofing the behavior against the D-parameters. The above may be considered components of distraction training. In the case of "take it" and "drop it," all four are applicable—as always, work through one at a time and relax the others (as well as adjusting the schedule of reinforcement) when increasing a parameter level.

Duration is a special case in training "drop it." Your goal is to administer the "drop it" cue, have the dog drop the item, and wait for an extended period of time, before "take it" is cued. This allows you to present the cue from a distance and cover that distance while the dog continues to wait without taking the toy back. Practice in close proximity first, and gradually increase the time between when the dog drops the item and you reinforce with the opportunity for the dog to take it again. Approaching the dog and item is likely to be a distraction, so work this aspect separately from duration training and then combine them afterward.

After duration is covered, work distance gradually and incrementally. Distance, as usual, involves presenting the evocative stimulus from further and further away from the dog.

Maintenance Stage
    Continue to expand proficiency. Ensure that you continue to use the cue and behavior on a regular basis in diverse environments, and to maintain or refine its features.

    You can work a sit into this sequence, if you like. To do this, cue drop it and then start cuing sit right away after the dog has dropped the item. Repeat through several trials and then delay the sit cue to see if sitting after dropping an item has been effectively conditioned. If so, reinforce and repeat. If not, perform several more trials before trying again.

    Generalize reinforcers. Begin using varied reinforcers, including games and toys, as well as everyday reinforcers like eating, going outside, meeting others, and investigating interesting things. If the item is an acceptable and safe item like a toy and not a curling iron or something, and it is the most effective reinforcer, use that rather than other more contrived reinforcers. Using other less effective reinforcers may function to punish dropping the item.

Loose-Leash Walking

    Loose-leash walking is another important behavior. It is difficult to enjoy walking with a dog who pulls on the leash. So, some owners are reluctant or refuse to walk their dog.

Behavior Objective
    Cue: Leash on.
    Behavior: Walking adjustment behaviors such that the shoulders stay within 1.8 meters of the handler—leash tightens at 1.8 meters indicating a non-criterion behavior.
    Consequence: Treats and forward progress.
    Criteria: Relative frequency: 100% through 10 trials; distance: maintain minimum 3 standard city blocks (approximately 425 meters); distraction: various (e.g., other dogs, other people, attractive objects like fire hydrants); diversity: parks, streets of all kinds.

Preliminaries
    Motivating operations & equipment. Start when the dog is hungry and not overly excited. It is likely that there are times when the dog will be less likely to pull. Try to identify these times and begin training then.

For instance, many dogs will pull less when they are walking indoors, rather than outside, or walking toward or away from home rather than the opposite, or after a good bout of exercise. Many dogs pull less in novel environments/neighborhoods. Work your way through a ranked list of increasingly challenging environments. This will help set both you and the dog up for success. It is best to begin in a minimally distracting room and move on to these other more challenging locations when you are assured of success. Have treats in a treat-pouch, ideally attached to your belt behind your back.

Before beginning, prevent pulling on the leash as much as possible in non-training session times. Every instance of pulling on the leash will make progress through the training process more challenging, because you will have to counter-condition it. If you must allow pulling on leash while you work to train loose-leash walking, consider using a standard buckle collar for those times and use a standard body harness for training and then after training. This is referred to as "discrimination training," as there are two distinct stimuli that indicate a differentiation between when pulling will be tolerated and when it will not. This will help protect your training progress.

Work with a 1.8-meter (six-foot) leash. I recommend that you use a standard body harness, rather than a neck collar, as this will reduce the "opposition reflex" (i.e., pulling against pressure, like when the barber tries to move your head and you have to put thought into moving your head rather than opposing it) that will challenge your training.

There are many ways to train loose-leash walking. One way is to emphasize a graded training approach.

Acquisition Stage

Prompt and reinforce the behavior. Begin by holding the leash with your dog seated or standing still beside you and facing the same direction. Press the hand that is clasping the leash up against your belt line and keep it in this position. This ensures that the distance to the end of the leash is a stable 1.8 meters at all times, and the distance will not be modified by your reach. You can place your thumb into your waistband. This acts as a quick release so that you don't get pulled over if the dog bolts for some reason—your thumb will come out of your waistband, and you'll have a brief interval in which to prepare to maintain your hold on the leash and prevent a sudden jerk on the leash. You can also use shock absorbing leashes such as the Larz leash (my personal favorite) to help reduce impacts on the dog (http://larzdogproducts.com/store/super-leashes/super-leash/).

Although being on leash will set the occasion (i.e., act as the cue) for walking close to you, a vocal cue such as "let's go" can be useful since the dog may interact with the environment on walks, and you will want a cue to proceed with walking. When initiating your movement, say "let's go," take a step forward, and as the dog begins to walk, click and treat after their first step. Repeat through several trials. (This procedure works well in most cases, but treats can be used to lure the walking if necessary.) Once this is smooth and reliable, set the criterion to two steps.

If the dog bolts forward at any point and the leash goes tight, stop moving forward and add as little stimulation as possible to the situation for several seconds. Evaluate whether you are moving too quickly through the task increments, and reduce the number of criterion steps if needed, to ensure that you minimize the number of such trials. Wait a few seconds and then proceed once the dog is not pulling on the leash. Continue to work in this manner, varying the criterion in a seemingly random manner, until you can get several loose-leash steps and very few non-criterion behaviors.

Use direction changes to help get more steps per trial and avoid non-criterion trials. Walking on a loose leash is really made up of a long series of modifications to walking behavior; the dog attends to your trajectory and speed, and these cues evoke the changes in their trajectory and speed. When you change directions, you encourage the dog to pay close attention to your location, and it puts you further ahead of them, which allows for a greater number of steps before they pull on the leash. It also increases interest. Once you have taken several steps and are getting to your current criterion limit, try changing directions at a 45– to 90–degree angle. Consider using a greater angle relative to how close the dog is to the end of the leash. For example, if the dog is still walking close to you, a slight change in direction can spice up the walk a bit, but if the dog is getting close to the end of the leash and the leash is about to go tight, use a wider angle, maybe even 90 degrees or more. Avoid jerking the leash though! This is **NOT** a leash "check"! *Gentle* pressure on the leash will come to cue the dog to pay attention to you for directional cues. This is easier for the dog when they are closer to you, so they can see you in their peripheral vision.

Fluency Stage

Fade food-in-hands. In most cases, you will not be using food as a lure and so there is no need to fade its use. However, some methods of training loose-leash walking can involve luring. In those cases, the process is similar, except that a lure is used to help generate the steps. In those cases, fade the food prompts at this point.

Manage session features. End sessions of a positive note. Use pace and enthusiasm as well as a high rate of reinforcement to ensure the dog's participation.

Establish a temporary cue. In the case of loose-leash walking, having the leash attached to the dog's collar or harness will come to serve as a permanent cue and no temporary cue is necessary. The vocalized "let's go" will also come to cue attention and walking on loose leash as you change directions are start walking.

Introduce a release cue. No specific vocal release cue will be necessary in this case, Removing the leash will come to serve as a release from loose-leash walking contingencies.

Thin the schedule of reinforcement. Begin gradually thinning the reinforcement schedule around a mean average but with no discernable pattern. You will go back to continuous reinforcement any time you increase the level of difficulty or introduce a new feature, and then gradually re-thin the schedule again.

Refine form, latency, and speed. Where necessary, refine each, one at a time, by gradually expecting a little closer of an approximation toward your goal (i.e., criterion). Maintain an expectation for any refinements made when you move on to work another (i.e., don't relax the criterion for what you have improved). In most cases, if the dog is not pulling on their leash, there is little need to refine these features.

Establish permanent cue. Putting on the leash and to vocal "let's go" will take on stimulus control from the beginning of training and serve as the permanent cue.

Proof against the D-parameters. Begin proofing the behavior against distraction, duration, distance, and diversity of environments, one at a time, relaxing the criteria for others when working one of them. Once each is to criterion individually, they may gradually be combined. Distance is not relevant in this case.

Training Dogs

Maintenance Stage

Continue to expand proficiency. Ensure you continue to "use" the cues and behavior on a regular basis in diverse environments, and to maintain or refine their features.

Generalize reinforcers. Begin using varied reinforcers, including games and toys as well as everyday reinforcers, meeting others, and investigating interesting things.

Special notes on loose-leash walking. A long and strong history of pulling on leash can be a major obstacle to training. In these cases, the same procedure discussed above can be used, but the progress will be much slower, and the training will take longer, because pulling will need to be extinguished. In some cases, an anti-pull harness might be worth considering, but avoid these where possible, focusing instead on arranging the environment and expectations to ensure success and reinforcing desired behaviors. In other words, tools won't train your dog—only you can do that, and tools that emphasize discomfort for problem behaviors are even less productive than tools that help you reinforce criterion behaviors. Don't be fooled by marketing; if a collar or harness is designed to tighten in any way on a dog when the dog pulls, then its use is based on aversive stimulation. Equipment can sometimes become necessary to get a "foot in the door," for particularly intractable problems, but they should be avoided where they are merely a crutch to avoid training. Rather than harnesses that are designed to tighten, usually under the armpits, in these cases, select ones that attach in the front as the mechanism which provides the added control. However, training will be more productive in the long run.

Some dogs hunker down like the proverbial "stubborn donkey" and refuse to move forward. They may or may not pull forward on leash at other times, but when a dog refuses to move forward, attempting to pull or otherwise force them forward, usually results in a longer battle.

Before starting training, it is important to first determine whether the dog may have medical problems, perhaps with arthritis or joint dysplasia, or perhaps the dog is heat-intolerant. Determine whether the dog seems fearful of something specific, and if so, avoid that situation while trying to train loose-leash walking. Address the fear reaction with a proper behavior change plan (the topic for book two in the *Dog Behavior* series). If the dog trails behind in specific situations, then perhaps a

85

previous experience with this situation was overwhelming or otherwise aversive. Force will only reinforce the problem.

If none the above factors appear to be an issue, be patient. Wait a few moments with a slack leash, and perhaps then gently verbally coax (prompt) the dog forward. If the dog does not respond to these attempts, discontinue coaxing, and begin a shaping program for moving forward.

First, be patient and have fun, *especially* at these times! Start by evoking a few other behaviors (e.g., down, sit, look, etc.) that you can reinforce and have fun with, perhaps including a game of tug. Start the actual shaping game by clicking and treating even the very slightest of forward motion. This might even have to be a slight relaxation of muscles or a slight shifting of weight. Once you have increased the rate of that miniscule amount of motion, expect just a little more during each successive set of trials, until the dog walks better on leash. Benefit is derived from not only achieving reinforcement opportunities, but also in that the added reinforcers will change any problematic emotional reactions occurring at that time. In other words, keeping up will simply become a lot more fun and nothing to fear! This shaping process is a slow process, no doubt about it. But it is the best solution and ought not be rushed. Try to have fun with it.

When the dog is exceptionally strong or large, compared to the person working with them, good training practices are even more important. Rather than manhandling the dog, identify and establish effective reinforcement. Carry out the training as described, but pay particular attention to ensuring successful trials, particularly with raising distraction levels. That said, this situation could be particularly challenging because if the dog does barge forward toward a distraction, the guardian may not be able to effectively ensure that reinforcement is blocked. Consider using an anti-pull harness for these situations. Avoid relying on anti-pull devices to make pulling aversive. Focus on controlling the dog's behavior with added reinforcers. However, for situations in which you simply cannot effectively control the dog, the anti-pull harness that operates by attaching the leash to the front of the chest as opposed to on the back may improve controllability. If the situation is extreme, then you should consider hiring a capable dog walker.

Your dog is just "crazy," you say? Although professional trainers, concerned with clarity, do not use such vague terms, trainers are quite familiar with the complaint that walking on leash is impossible, because the dog is "crazy." Specify exactly what actual behaviors the dog exhibits and what cues are controlling them. This encompasses various scenarios such as a dog that expends extensive energy engaging in many behaviors rapidly (e.g., bolting in different directions, chewing at the leash, bouncing, or jumping). The key element is that the dog rapidly engages in numerous and various non-criterion behaviors. This is common with some puppies and dogs new to leashes, or dogs with bodies in an activity-deprived state. It can also be common with dogs that are fearful. These non-criterion behaviors function to self-distract or escape something.

If the dog is new to leashes, introduce the leash slowly, and shape tolerance-related behaviors with increasing contact with the collar and leash. If the dog is fearful, find a professional animal behavior technologist/consultant to help you resolve the problem, and come back to loose-leash walking when you can. Or, find a time and place where you are able to avoid or bypass these behaviors. Book two in the *Dog Behavior* series will address such challenges.

If it turns out that the problem is associated with excess stimulation, find a minimally arousing environment for the initial stages of training walking on a loose leash. Work in increasingly arousing environments as part of proofing for distraction practices. Carry out the training after an extensive exercise or play session, or identify times when the problem is less likely to occur. Exercise is commonly very helpful in these situations. In any case, arrange to set the dog up for success as much as possible and maintain the basic strategies of training. Make the behavior you want more likely and other behaviors less likely, set the criteria low, and gradually and incrementally work your way through the levels of difficulty with a graded training approach. Try to avoid participating in the "craziness" and instead be calm, contributing as little stimulation and reinforcement as possible to the situation when the dog is acting "crazy." Consider cuing a few other behaviors and calmly reinforcing them, if you believe you can get the dog to exhibit the behaviors in the presence of the distraction. Reinforce any instances of calmness in a calm way. In this way, you will shape calmness and participation in walking. Ensure the process is a calm type of fun for the dog.

Training Dogs

Chapter 7. Training Challenges and Special Cases

In this final chapter, we explore a few common training challenges. The information in this chapter and the previous one are covered in my book, *The Science and Technology of Animal Training*, but it was written for a professional audience.

Multi-Dog Training

Karen London and Patricia McConnell (2001) wrote a terrific book called *Feeling Outnumbered? How to Manage and Enjoy Your Multi-Dog Household*, in which they outline a basic strategy for working with dogs who reside together. London and McConnell outlined an approach that has proven very successful for many trainers, myself included, over the years. I outline this general approach below.

Train Each Dog Individually

Arrange to have time alone with each dog for training. This can be incorporated into walks and play sessions, or exercise sessions as well as training. With multiple dogs providing a significant distraction for each other, it can be challenging to compete with the presence of multiple dogs, and soon, cues lose their capacity to evoke behaviors, even those behaviors that were previously well trained. Thus, it is best to initially train each dog individually.

Ensure that the dog's name precedes all other cues; when training an individual dog this is rarely necessary. This begins the discrimination training that will carry on when you begin training multiple dogs together. Names are simply cues evoking attention and so using the individual dog's name will eventually result in the named dog alone exhibiting the cued behavior. Begin using the dog's name during individual training to establish the name as the cue for attention.

Train in Pairs

Once you are at a reliable point in individual training, you may start training the dogs in pairs. Start by training in pairs even if you have several dogs. Ensure you precede cues with the dogs' names. Carry out much the same training as you did with the dogs individually, but review it with the other dogs who are present, so that each dog exhibits the behavior that you cue and other dogs do not.

Once you begin working with more than one dog, use the dog's name, followed by the cue, as described above, and reinforce the occurrence of the behavior from *only* that dog and *not* others. Over time, discrimination will occur. At first, other dogs may respond to the cues, but discrimination will occur when you fail to reinforce responses that were not preceded with *their* name, and the named dog will exhibit the behavior while other dogs will be less likely to do so.

You can also work on group cues, using a group name, such as "Everyone," followed by the primary cue. Only those dogs who exhibit the behavior are given treats and the same discrimination process occurs. This group cue will come in handy when you want all the dogs to respond similarly together. For instance, it can be useful to be able to evoke sit from all of the dogs or to get them all to come to you when playing together or with others in a park.

Train in Groups

Once you have worked your way through training each pair combination to a reliable level of distraction, you can start working with combinations of three dogs. The training will proceed in much the same way as with pairs. Once significant progress has been made in these small groups, in each possible combination of three, you can start adding in any other dogs within the household, until you have your whole group working together. Continue to work with the dogs individually and as a group, and applying the training to everyday life when possible.

Training Toy Breeds

Toy breed dogs are frequently fearful, especially when close to people walking around, because they are at significant risk of being stepped on and potentially injured. Consider at least administering the acquisition stage of training while you are seated on the ground next to the dog, both to prevent emotional arousal from moving around near them, but also to get closer to the dog in order to perform lures and effectively deliver reinforcers. This will need to be faded.

Another challenge with training some toy breed dogs, is not really a challenge with the dog him or herself, but rather with the owner. Because it is usually so easy to physically manipulate toy breed dogs, people frequently do not train their toy breed dogs. Some people simply fail to recognize that there is a reason to do so, while others find it challenging because of the dog's size. Lack of training is likely a major reason for the stereotype of the "snappy and yappy" toy breed dog. People fail to take these and other problem behaviors or lack of training as a serious problem. It is important to recognize the need for basic training. Being "snappy and yappy" is *not* inevitable for toy breed dogs. A well-trained toy breed dog is a joy to be around.

Social Contact not an Effective Reinforcer

For some individuals, social contact is not an effective reinforcer, and this can affect training quite dramatically—people become quite used to utilizing social reinforcement. People often tend to identify a treat as the reinforcer for a behavior they want to train, but reinforcement is frequently a package of stimuli, including the social contact that comes with exhibiting social behaviors (e.g., during training) and receiving the reinforcer. Even if praise or touch are not used during training, and vocal and visual prompts are not used either (they frequently are), the social contact that otherwise accompanies training contributes to generating and reinforcing behaviors. With this major motivating operation reduced or eliminated, training can be more challenging.

A history of aversive conditioning can overshadow the effectiveness of social reinforcement. Furthermore, a lack of effective early socialization can prevent social contact from becoming reinforcing. There might also be genetic influences on the effectiveness of social reinforcement. If the dog lacks a history of effective socialization, remedial socialization may help. If the dog has a history of aversive conditioning mediated by humans, a careful rehabilitation will be required. In either case (remedial socialization or rehabilitation), gradual graded added reinforcement can increase the effectiveness of social contact as a reinforcer. Generally, you can improve social motivation by reinforcement-rich, non-coercive social interaction.

Hand feeding of favored treats and food can often help. Participate in games and other reinforcing activities. End sessions on a positive note, before the dog becomes excessively satiated with the contact. Leave the dog "wanting more," so to speak. Try to become a source of more reinforcement for the dog in general, without overdoing it. As social motivation increases, training should become more fun and productive for both the dog and trainer.

Food is not an Effective Reinforcer

For many dogs, food is simply not a very effective reinforcer. In many cases, you can find better quality treats and mildly deprive the dog of these more effective reinforcers to maximize their effectiveness. If this does not increase the effectiveness of the treat as a reinforcer, consider other reinforcers such as contact with a favored toy or perhaps a quick game of tug. For some dogs, praise and certain specific kinds of physical contact can be an effective reinforcer. You may need to experiment with different kinds of social contact to determine what is reinforcing for your dog. Usually, gentle to moderate contact on a shoulder or chest works well and pats on the head do not. Observe what the dog expends significant energy contacting on a daily basis for reinforcers, including getting dinner and going outside. Once you have a list of effective reinforcers, consider *mild* deprivation to increase their effectiveness.

Hyperactivity

Some dogs are so hyperactive that it becomes a significant disruption to training. This is common with certain breeds and with puppies/adolescents. The most common solution for this problem is exercise, manipulation of excess stimulation during training, and shaping focus, attention, and calmness. In many cases, owners can increase exercise without the help of a fitness consultant, as long as they operate within the medical and biological limitations of their dog, and increase the dog's exercise level gradually. The sessions should be scheduled regularly and ideally involve games to make things fun. Ensure warm-ups and cool-downs, and observe carefully for indications of fatigue. You might notice some benefits of moderate to intense appropriately implemented exercise programs after only a few sessions, but you will recognize most of the stable physiological benefits after several weeks of regular exercise. Try to train during times of the day that are most conducive to concentration as well.

In addition to the benefits of physical conditioning, behavioral conditioning can also help. You can improve focus in general with training games and puzzles that emphasize patience and focus, as well as creativity and persistence in general.

General Sensitivity and Risk Aversion

Dogs, who are generally sensitive and risk-averse, require a careful approach to training. Trainers need to attend to and recognize escape contingencies and sensitivities, so that they can avoid these forms of stimulation while working through training. In some cases, dogs are sensitive to social pressure and cower when someone towers over or approaches them. In these cases, train while sitting beside the dog, perhaps right on the ground. Face slightly away and avoid staring at the dog. Avoid sudden movements and be calm, but gently praising. Train in a calm environment that you are sure you can control. Take extra care to avoid aversive stimulation, such as techniques involving extinction or subtracted punishment trials. Ensure success by moving at an appropriate pace. Set the dog up for success. Utilize a very careful graded and errorless approach, and begin introducing simple shaping exercises with minimal prompts. Generally, this kind of shaping can reinforce creativity, persistence, and resilience in general. Severe cases may require a full behavior change program, designed by a behaviorologist or professional animal behavior technologist.

Easily Frustrated and Impulsive

Frustration refers to the blocked access to reinforcers and the emotional arousal elicited by extinction. *Impulsivity* refers to the tendency for a dog to seek out immediate smaller reinforcers when faced with the opportunity to engage in different behaviors that generate different reinforcers (something we call "concurrent contingencies") and delayed access to a much greater source of reinforcement. Dogs tend to go for the "quick fix," rather than putting in slightly more time and effort for much greater gratification.

One must carefully handle dogs that are impulsive and easily frustrated. They can be conditioned to delay gratification and experience less frustration, if the contingencies are suitably arranged. The trick here is to take a graded training approach, specifically with regard to the effort the dog must expend to contact the reinforcer and the duration features of training. Gradually, train behaviors that require duration, but move at a pace that allows the dog to succeed in contacting highly effective reinforcers that require a bit more effort and time. Similarly, use shaping exercises with minimal prompting, to condition the creativity and persistence that will allow the dog to easily work through and around frustrations. By emphasizing success generated by creativity and persistence, the dog will begin to respond to frustration with other novel productive behaviors and strategies that will access the reinforcer, rather than non-criterion behaviors. It is also likely that the dog will begin to really enjoy training!

References

Arden, A. (1999). *Train Your Dog the Lazy Way*. New York: Alpha Books.

Goldiamond, I. (2002). Toward a Constructional Approach to Social Problems: Ethical and Constitutional Issues Raised by Applied Behavior Analysis. *Behavior and Social Issues.* Retrieved from http://www.bfsr.org/BSI_11_2/11_2Gold.pdf

London, K. B., & McConnell, P. B. (2001). *Feeling Outnumbered? How to Manage and Enjoy Your Multi-Dog Household*. Black Earth: Dog's Best Friend, Ltd.

O'Heare, J. (2016). *Canine Separation Anxiety Workbook*. Ottawa, Canada: BehaveTech Publishing.

Pryor, K. W., Haag, R., & O'Reilly, J. (1969). The Creative Porpoise: Training for Novel Behavior. *Journal of the Experimental Analysis of Behavior, 12* (4), 653–661.

Sidman, M. (2001). *Coercion and its Fallout* (Revised ed.). Boston: Author's Cooperative, Inc. Publishers.

Zink, C. (1997). *Peak Performance: Coaching the Canine Athlete* (2nd. ed.). Lutherville: Canine Sports Productions.

Index